CW00864716

Casting Spells *and* Talking to the Goddess

Kardia Zoe

DEDICATION

This book is dedicated to you, my reader. You are my true source of inspiration and motivation to continue writing. I love sharing my insight into Wicca and the Old Ways with you and it is my hope that you'll experience the same magic on this path that I do. If you find the information I share helpful, please help others find this book by leaving a review for it on Amazon. Thanks so much!

Peace and health be with you,
Kardia

ACKNOWLEDGMENTS

Unless otherwise noted, the quotes in this book are all from a series of books known as the *Essene Gospel of Peace*. These ancient writings were t*ranslated and edited by EDMOND BORDEAUX SZEKELY*.

Other information published in this book draws from our popular Living Wicca Today e-publications, articles Kardia has written over the past 15 years for the Inner Circle newsletter and material written for our website:
http://wicca.com

CONTENTS

Part 1 Wicca A Beginner's Guide To Casting Spells

Working with Herb, Crystal and Candle Magic

Getting Started

Do you think casting spells is hard or complicated? Have you avoided this aspect of Wicca because you were worried you'd make a mistake? Perhaps you tried casting a spell in the past that simply did not work and now you think spell casting is something that only happens in the movies.

A Beginner's Guide to Casting Spells is not a book of prewritten spells. Instead, it will help the beginner understand the Universal Laws that ultimately determine whether spells succeed or fail. If you want to go beyond the lists of ingredients and to do steps, to learn what actually makes your spells work, this book is for you.

You'll receive guidance on how to use magical tools, herbs, crystals and candles to create powerful spells that enrich your life and improve the world around you. This is a must-read book if you're a beginner who wants to cast spells with confidence and experience the magic of the Universe in a new way!

In the first part of this book you'll gain a clear understanding of the Universal Laws that determine the success or failure of your spells. Next you'll learn what types of spells are best, which you should avoid, and how to train you mind to get the results you want.

Part 2 of this book will introduce you to basic candle magic and teach you how to work with crystals and stones. A fairly comprehensive reference guide is also provided to help you learn the traditional magical energies of common plants and herbs used in spellwork.

I would like to note that it took me several years to fully understand what spells were and how they worked. I was raised as a Christian and grew up thinking casting spells was an ungodly thing to do. As I began to explore Wicca, I imagined that spells were a lot like prayers, but a few old practitioners corrected me. Most who cast spells put a considerable amount of energy into them. This of course amplifies the results, so it is vital that you have accurate knowledge of the Laws and are clear about what you are doing.

Regardless of your current situation, you can achieve whatever you think and believe you can. Simply follow the Universal Laws outlined in this book.

The power of the Divine has always been within you. Most people believe they are at the mercy of the Universe and think there is nothing they can do to change what happens in their lives. This is simply not true! The Universe is constantly responding to your requests, but there are Laws you must understand and obey.

After reading this book you'll have a solid understanding of what you need to do to cast spells successfully and how to create the spells that help you reach your personal goals. If you are ready, let's get started!

Dealing With The Spell Casting Controversy

Casting spells is a controversial topic. Some believe this activity should be left to advanced practitioners. Others feel it is a way to communicate with the Universe and they provide newcomers with books of spells for every occasion.

While I agree that casting spells is a wonderful way to send energy out to the Universe, I understand the concern of those who guard this practice. It is essential that you master some key Universal Laws if you want your spells to work properly.

Too often beginners do not have a good understanding of these Laws or they are completely unaware of them! They buy a spellbook or two, gather the ingredients listed and jump right in. Certainly we would all like it if our spells worked instantly to improve our finances, bring back a lost love or solve some other challenge in our life. But spells don't really work that way.

The magic that you work with comes from within. When you cast a spell, you are drawing that energy out and sending the Universe a request. Learning to control your thoughts and feelings so that you send the right energy out is not always easy for beginners. It takes practice to master this and thus, most seasoned practitioners believe beginners should take their time.

Some find spell casting easy, but most will need months, if not years to truly master this craft. So be patient. As you learn and apply the Universal Laws in this book, you will be well on your way to living a life full of magic!

The journey of a thousand miles starts with one step. Lao-Tzu

Why Some Spells Work And Others Don't

A solid understanding of the Universal Laws and a strong belief in your own ability to draw what you need into your life is essential in spell work. In the movies we are often given the impression that having the right candles, oils and herbs will cause magical things to happen. In reality, the ingredients are simply tools that the practitioner uses to help draw out the power from within. The results depend less on the ingredients than they do on an individual's ability to focus and send forth the proper energy.

You don't need to follow a written spell exactly for it to work. Practitioners frequently change ingredients and add their own personal touch. A beginner would be wise to concentrate on the type of energy they are sending out first and then add the helpful components to their spells slowly as they learn to control their thoughts and feelings. As you begin to understand how the Universal Laws work, you'll be amazed at how simple and effective casting spells can be!

Most Wiccans follow the Wiccan Rede. The Rede is a statement that outlines the key moral system in the religion of Wicca and certain other related Witchcraft-based faiths. The word "Rede" comes from Middle English, meaning "advice" or "counsel". You will often see the Rede summed up with the words "An it harm none, do what ye will". This teaching is simple. If an action causes no harm to anyone, there is no Divine law against it. This includes YOU. Behavior that is harmful to your own well-being violates the Rede. Simply keep all your actions helpful, not hurtful and you are obeying the Wiccan Rede. You can find the full version of the Rede at: http://wicca.com/celtic/wicca/rede.htm

Another very important Law is the Wiccan Law of Three, or the Three-fold Law. Today, this is more commonly known as the Law of

Attraction. This is actually the Law that determines the outcome of your spell. It is what responds to the energy you send out. It's essential to consider this Law in all your spell casting, because spells are basically a concentrated form of energy. You certainly don't want to send out negative energy and have it returned to you three-fold!

Actually, this happens a lot. The Universal Law responds to ALL thoughts and feelings being sent out, no matter who you are or what you believe. People are manifesting things into their life every day. Unfortunately, most are manifesting what they DON'T want in their lives because they don't understand how this law works.

For example, those who need additional income for paying bills often try to do a money spell. They buy a spell book or two, gather all the ingredients and follow all the steps in their prewritten spell, hoping that this will bring them the money they need. But instead of extra money coming into their life, they receive more bills! Why? Because when they cast the spell, they were feeling broke and lacking. This is the energy they sent out to the Universe, so this is what multiplied and returned to them.

Spells for improving health are also challenging for the beginner. We all want more energy and vibrant health. However, too often those who ask the Universe to improve their health, are actually sending out feelings of being tired and ill. The Universe will always return more of the same feelings to you.

To get the response from the Universe you want, you must send clear messages through your thoughts AND feelings. You can't send one message with your thoughts or words (I want more money) and then send another through your feelings (I feel broke) because if you do this, your FEELINGS will always override your thoughts and the Universe will faithfully send you more reasons to feel broke.

Most of us have heard how important positive thinking is to our success. I'll tell you right now, if you think positive thoughts won't help you, you are probably right! Thinking about something will not automatically make it happen. Your thoughts have to generate intense feelings or a sincere desire for what you want.

Thoughts are very powerful, but it's your feelings and actions, not your words, that speak volumes! Use the power of your thoughts to visualize your goals until you can actually *feel* what it is like to achieve them. When your thoughts and feelings are in sync, you are sending a clear message to the Universe and things may start to happen quickly!

If you can recognize and control the type of energy you send out in your spells, you will always get the results you want. The next chapter will help you consistently create the positive spells you want and avoid negative results.

Spells That Beginners Need To Avoid

In this chapter I will help you determine the types of spells that will get you the results you want. But first, I want to share a few important guidelines you must follow to ensure the spells you cast bring you positive results.

Spell Casting Tips to Remember:

1. You are working WITH the natural energies within and around you, not trying to control them.
2. Focus on casting spells for intangible goals. Qualities like self-confidence, vibrant health, peace, happiness, wisdom and love will always open the door to a steady flow of new blessings.
3. Only cast spells on yourself. Never try to influence the free will of another with magic. If you attempt to harm or influence a person or situation in any way, you will only draw that type of energy back into your own life.
4. You should be aware of your true thoughts AND feelings at all times, but it's especially important to when you are doing spell work. If you want to draw positive energy and blessings into your life, you MUST send out that type of energy in your spells.

Here's a few examples of positive, intangible goals:

If you want to increase your income, cast a spell that helps you FEEL rich. If you simply ask the Divine to send you money, there will likely be feelings of lack and need attached to your request, which can only result in more lack and need being returned to you. Instead, think about all the little blessings you have already receive in your life and send out energy to express your gratitude. The Universe will always respond to this by sending you more to be thankful for!

If you want to improve your health, visualize what it feels like to have abundant energy and vibrant health., then send out feelings of gratitude for all the things you can still do. Again, you are sure to discover an increase in your energy and health as the Universe helps you find ways to multiply your feelings of well-being.

If you are thinking about casting a love spell on someone, you may want to reconsider. This usually involves another person's free-will which goes against the Wiccan Rede. Instead of casting a love spell on someone else, why not cast a spell on yourself to increase your attractiveness?

The webmaster of wicca.com wrote a wonderful article that offers guidance on casting love spells. It is reprinted here with permission to help you understand why these type of spells should be avoided.

Love Spells by Herne

The primary question one must consider before undertaking any ritual working, especially where Love Magic is concerned is, *Is This Working Consistent With The Basic Tenant of HARM NONE as expressed in The Rede.

Upon asking yourself the following two questions, you can effectively analyze the reasons to either justify or dismiss the working.

1. *What is my intent in performing this work?*
2. *Is this spell or ritual influenced by anger; hatred; lust; greed; jealousy or envy?*

If your answer to question number 1 is found within question number 2, then as a Wiccan and follower of the Light Path, you must abandon this spell or ritual because it will not be consistent with the Rede.

Likewise, if question 1 is answered by question 2 and you continue, you can no longer rightfully call yourself Wiccan. A True Wiccan will not use manipulative magic to negatively influence another for their own personal interests. The whole purpose of following this path is to live in harmony and balance with the natural rhythms of life, not to manipulate them to suit a selfish goal. At this point, you need to refer to yourself as a follower of the Dark Path since manipulative magic for personal gain without consideration of the outcome falls within that realm...

Harsh words? You betcha... Does it make you uncomfortable? Good...

By undertaking such an action without the consent or approval of another, you are clearly disregarding the Rede and using your gifts for purely selfish reasons. Therefore, you are setting forces in motion which will ultimately have negative impact in one way or another and you are practicing Dark Magic.

You must remember that once you create and release this energy as a thought form, it will acquire life, form and substance. It will run its course, and the final outcome through the laws of cause and effect may not be what you wanted. The potential for great harm to both yourself and others are clearly evident in such a working. This is especially clear when you consider that you will eventually need to absorb this energy back into yourself after it has ruined your life and the lives of who knows how many others...

...I caution you that nonconsensual Love Magic is a double edged sword and borders on the manipulation of another human being against their *Free Will.* It is also dangerously close to Psychic Rape and is considered highly unethical by most who practice the Craft.

I hope this has given those who have considered using such practices food for thought. While my opinion may not be shared by all, it illustrates the need to consider all potential outcomes before focusing and releasing a spell.

It is clear in this article that you should never direct a Love Spell towards anyone who is not aware of the spell or has not consented to you working it. Instead, simply construct your spell or ritual so that you draw the ideal mate into your life. This is different than using magic to make someone fall in love with you, as you are not trying to influence a specific person's free will.

Develop a list of qualities, attributes and interests that you seek in the ideal mate. After you've done this, research the appropriate herbs, oils and or magical tools needed for this type of spell and focus on drawing love into your life. As with all magic, results take time, focus and energy. What you get back from the spell will totally depend on the energy you put into it. It is a ritual you'll need to repeat on a regular basis until it manifests in your life.

Have enough confidence in and respect for yourself to know that you deserve to be loved and it will come to you when the time is right. Give nature a chance to work its own spell. You must remember that Magic is not for the impatient.

In the end, putting energy and effort into being attentive, considerate, seductive, romantic and showing genuine interest and desire for one another is the greatest love magic there is.

To sum things up for you, never cast a spell that will control the free-will of another or cause harm in any way. This will bring negative energy into your life as well.

Don't ask the Divine for material things. Instead, focus on the intangible qualities you would like to multiply in your life.

Avoid sending feeling of want and need into the Universe. They will only be returned to you three-fold.

Finally, keep your thoughts and feelings positive at all times. The Universe is responding to you every minute of every day, not just during your spell work!

The Most Powerful Ingredient In Spells

Simply relying on the right color candle, correct incense or special herbs to work their magic will leave you wondering what you left out. The special ingredient you may have left out is YOU!

I decided to write this book because our website received so many emails over the years from beginners complaining that they had followed a spell EXACTLY as it was written, and it failed to work. They wanted to know what they were doing wrong. Like most of us, they had seen movies or TV shows that suggested having the right combination of colored candles, special herbs, oils and magical words would solve their financial or relationship problems. They did not understand that the ingredients in their spell was only a small part of the process.

Most books on casting spells only give you half of the information you really need. You are given lists of ingredients and action steps, but no explanation of how or why these spells really work. The Universal Laws that govern the results are not clearly explained and the new practitioner is left with only a vague understanding of what they are doing.

This is a problem, as those who are truly interested in manifesting their desires are not adding the most important ingredient, or worse yet, they are adding the wrong ingredient. That ingredient is the personal energy that they send out. This is what the Universe will ultimately respond to.

Personal energy is the key ingredient in all spells. If you have ever asked your mom or a friend for a recipe because you wanted to make the same meal they made, only to have that recipe fail when you tried to duplicate it, you probably understand what I am talking about. Even when you follow their recipe exactly as it was written, it never seems to turn out the same for you. Their personal touch will always be missing. A good cook will simply add a little of his or her energy to the recipe and make it their own.

11

Like a favorite recipe, sometimes you may need to modify a spell just a little to make it work for you. Changing the color of a candle or using a different scent of incense will not make the Divine angry or cause the Universe to ignore you. If you are sending out thoughts and feelings that are positive and full of gratitude, your spells will always return positive results.

If you already have a shelf full of spell books and have collected all the right ingredients for a spell, that's great! But if you are just starting out or are missing what seems to be key ingredients, don't let it be a major concern. The Universe will be responding to YOU, not your collection of herbs, oils or crystals.

Okay, now let's talk about how your magical tools really work...

How Magical Tools Enhance Your Spells

Magic would not be complete without scented oils, homemade magical brews and smoke rising from the incense as it carries our thoughts up into the universe. We weave spells utilizing the simple but potent powers found within the tools nature gives us. The power of incense and oils can magically transform our lives.

Magic can be as simple as rubbing scented oil on a colored candle, setting it in a holder and lighting it as you visualize your magical need. Or it can be more complex, involving several candles, many oils, incense, ritual clothing, chants and more. The details are up to you. What's important is that you use Magic to bring light, joy and peace into your life and the world around you.

By now you should understand that all magic comes from within. Your magical tools simply help you draw out the thoughts and feelings that you want to send out to the Universe.

Most Wicca beginner books will tell you about common tools like your athame, cauldron, wand, chalice and so on. I already covered those tools in book #2 of this series, A Beginner's Guide to Earth Magic, so in this book, I'll simply share how these tools work to enhance your results.

To help you understand their true purpose of your tools, I am going to share an excerpt from book #2. It clearly describes the benefits and is worth repeating here:

Think back to a time when you dressed up for a job interview or an important social event. What you wore made you feel better about yourself, and thus improved your chances for a successful outcome. You knew that your clothes didn't really have magical powers, but there was no question that having the right outfit and accessories boosted your self-confidence, and THAT is why these items were needed.

Magical tools work the same way. They are a part of our rituals because they can help us focus our thoughts and generate the ideal atmosphere to work in.

Incense can create a magical atmosphere that helps you achieve the desired mental state for your ritual. It can be used both on and off the altar to cleanse and create sacred space. If for any reason the smoke of incense bothers you, essential oil can work as a substitute. But be sure to include one or the other. *The effects of aroma can have a significant impact on any rituals or magical work.*

Stones or crystals may also be used in your spell work. You'll find a list of their traditional magical properties in the second half of this book. I simply wanted to stress here that stones are easy to carry with you and are a great little reminder of the beautiful gifts our Mother Earth wants to share with you.

Herbs are another example of the many blessings our Mother Earth offers us. It's very common to see them listed in spells, but we should be using them in our daily life as well. Whenever I consume living foods, I think about the life-energy of the food entering my body and merging with my own. Spiritual leaders from many different paths also believe that living foods (fresh fruits and vegetables) actually enhance our ability to communicate with the Divine. If this is true, then consuming Mother Earth's living foods can help raise physical, mental and spiritual energy and should be considered an important part of all magical practice.

Finally, you might not think of jewelry as being a "tool" for magical work. However, placing a small pentacle or symbol of your beliefs on your alter or simply carrying it around with you throughout the day, is also a great little reminder of the power that is within you.

One Tool You Should Never Be Without

A Book of Shadows (BOS) is one of the most important tools a Witch has. Some have been passed down through Covens or from one individual to another, but today most are written by solitary practitioners. It's basically your magical diary or journal, where you record all your experiences, rituals, spells and lore. Think of it as a photo album of your magical journey. Every time you make an entry, your words create a "snapshot" of where you are. As you explore your path and discover what works best for you, your book will grow. You'll be preserving the details of your communication with the Divine, and creating a chronicle of your journey ... your own personal grimoire.

NOTE: A grimoire is like a Book of Shadows, but not as personal. If you want to keep a BOS and a grimoire, put information about rituals, celebrations, spells, and the magical properties of objects in your Grimoire, and record personal information, like thoughts, feelings, and ideas, in your BOS. This allows you to share magical entries with a witch friend, without her reading all your personal entries.

Your BOS can be a three-ring notebook, a bound blank book, or even a folder on your computer. Some use a nice hardbound book for their BOS and keep their grimoire in a notebook so they can add or remove pages. Others use their computer to record everything. The advantages of a computer are that you don't have to worry about making mistakes in your entries, and you can add images or information you download from the Internet. Use whatever works best for you!

Start your Book of Shadows by entering your current feelings about this path. Write down the reasons you think Wicca is right for you. What are your goals? What do you hope to achieve and learn? What do you fear about following this path? How do you see the Goddess and God? Let all your thoughts and feelings out here, this is a private book and nobody else will ever read it. There are no right or wrong answers and it is not a test. It is simply a way to help you define your understanding of this path, and later on, it will help you see how far you have come on your journey!

Preparing Yourself For Casting Spells

When you practice any type of magic you are sending out concentrated forms of energy and this can have an effect on the entire world around you, so act responsibly. Remember the Wiccan Rede "An it harm none, do what ye will" when you are creating your spell. Always keep in mind that any magical energy you send out will return to you three fold, whether it is positive or negative.

Prior to your ritual or magical work, prepare yourself a nice relaxing bath. Add a hand full of sea salt to get your charges set where they need to be. Light a few candles, turn off the light and relax. Clear your mind of the junk you have picked up throughout the day. Showers can also help refresh your spirit. Visualize the water washing all the negativity away from you. Your mind should be at ease and clear prior to any spell working.

Many practitioners ground themselves before spell work to release any negative energy they may have picked up earlier in the day. You can read more about the practice of grounding, casting circles and energy work in book 2 of the Living Wicca Today series, Wicca: *A Beginner's Guide to Earth Magic*.

If you simply approach spell work with a positive attitude and send forth only the energy you want to see multiplied in your life, you'll always achieve the results you want.

Candle Magic Basics

Candle Magic has been around for many years. It's an easy, yet powerful form of magic that can help you apply the energies of the body with the powers of the mind to obtain your desires. Some candle magic may have to be repeated over a period of days. Therefore, you will want to place your candles in an area that will not be disturbed. It's best to avoid rooms with a TV, radio noise or disturbances of any kind. Candle magic should be performed in a low traffic area whenever possible. A bedroom is often ideal for such work.

As with all magical tools, the candle made by the practitioner for a specific purpose captures the energy of the practitioner. Some prefer to work with beeswax candles, as they believe these are more powerful because they are produced from nature. But any type of candles can be used for candle magic. Just remember to cleanse and consecrate them prior to use.

Cleansing removes all the negative energies that the candle may have picked up along the way. You want your candles to be as free of psychic debris as possible. Submerge the candle in salt (sea salt if possible) and then ask the God and Goddess to bless it. No formal words or ritual is needed. Simply speak from your heart.

Many Wiccans like to dress their candle with oil. Use whatever oil you prefer. If your candle will be burned to bring something to you, rub the oil on the candle in a downward motion from the top to the middle and then from the bottom to the middle. To send something away from you, rub the oil from the middle of the candle out to the ends. Never make a back and forth motion as this defeats the purpose. Dab the remaining oil from your fingers onto your third eye and on your breastbone. Then say the following:

"I cleanse and consecrate this candle in the name of the God and Goddess. May it burn with strength in the service of the light."

State and/or visualize your intent for the candle as you light it.

Some will also inscribe their candle with a name or word to represent its purpose. If you have an Athame, you can use it to inscribe your candle. The same principle as dressing the candle is used. To draw something to you, write from the top to the middle, and then from the bottom to the middle. To repel things, write from the middle to the ends.

Below is a list of traditional candle colors used in magic, with a brief description of their most common magical uses. White candles can be used as a substitute for any color. Keep lots on hand!

Traditional Candle Colors for Spell Casting

White: The Goddess, Higher Self, Purity, Peace, Virginity

Black: Binding, Shapeshifting, Protection, Repels Negativity

Brown: Special Favors, To Influence Friendships

Purple: Third Eye, Psychic Ability, Hidden Knowledge, To Influence People in High Places, Spiritual Power

Blue: Element of Water, Wisdom, Calm, Protection, Good Fortune, Opening Blocked Communication, Spiritual Inspiration

Green: The Element of Earth, Physical Healing, Monetary success, Tree and Plant Magic, Growth, Personal Goals

Pink: Affection, Romance, Caring, Nurturing, Good Will

Red: Element of Fire, Passion, Strength, Fast action, Career Goals, Lust, Driving Force, Survival, Blood of the Moon

Orange: General Success, Property Deals, Legal matters, Justice, Selling

Yellow: The Element of Air, the Sun, Mental Energies, Intelligence, Memory, Logical Imagination. Use to Accelerate Learning and Break Mental Blocks.

This was a very magical room! The Magical Store owner from the Celtic Connection is standing with some beautiful Amethyst cathedrals at a local supplier. These amazing gifts of Mother Earth took my breath away!

Working With Crystals & Gemstones

Over the centuries various Gemstones, Crystals and certain rock formations have held a great mystical appeal to humans. We have found beauty, power, and mystery within stones. Our ancestors knew and understood the spiritual, magical and healing properties of gemstones and crystals, but that wisdom was nearly forgotten over time.

In the past, mystic properties of stones were unquestioned. They were commonly used in magical rituals to help focus the mind and attune the user with the powers that created the Earth and everything on it. Today a few still associate various stones with the four elements, Earth, Air, Fire, and Water. Some of the more common associations are listed below.

Element of Earth - Traditional Stones Include: Emerald, Green Jade, Green Tourmaline, Agate, Black Tourmaline, Hematite, Jasper, Malachite, Onyx, Obsidian, Peridot, Quartz, Salt (all types)

Element of Air - Traditional Stones Include: Opal, Tiger Eye, Citrine, Topaz, Turquoise, Diamond and Zircon

Element of Fire: Traditional Stones Include - Amber, Carnelian, Citrine, Fire Agate, Fire Opal, Garnet, Red Calcite, Red Jasper, Red Tourmaline, Ruby, Sunstone

Element of Water: Traditional Stones Include - Amethyst, Aquamarine, Azurite, Moonstone, Azurite, Blue Calcite, Blue Lace Agate, Blue Topaz, Celestite, Chalcedony, Chrysocolla, Lapis Lazuli, Pearl, Sapphire, Sodalite, Sea Salt

NOTE: For additional reading on elemental magic we recommend *Wicca Elemental Magic* by Lisa Chamberlain.

Caring for Your Crystals

Crystals and gemstones can pick up negative or unwanted energies over time. Below are several methods you can use to clear crystals and stones of negative energies and restore them to their natural vibrant energy.

1. Place your Crystals in dry sea salt for up to 24 hours to clear them of unwanted energies. Stones can also be stored in sea salt to keep them from picking up negative energies from their surroundings.

2. The rays of the Sun or Moon can also be used to clear and recharge your Crystals and stones. Place them outside or in a window where they can soak up the sunlight or moonlight. Some stones may fade in prolonged sun exposure. If you have any doubts at all, it may be best to use only moonlight cleansing.

3. Smudging is one of the fastest and easiest methods of clearing crystals and stones of unwanted energy. Simply pass your stone several times through the smoke of a smudge stick or incense. Favorite smudge sticks include cedar, sage and/or sweetgrass.

 4. Burying crystals and stones in the soft Earth for 3 days to a week is another way to cleanse them. You can bury them in your yard or in a flower pot. The Earth will naturally absorb negative energy and neutralize it.

A Brief Guide To Using Crystals & Stones

In this section you'll find a convenient list of commonly used stones with their traditional magical uses and a little folklore. For a more extensive list and additional information on crystals and gemstones, visit: http://wicca.com/celtic/stones/stones0.htm

AMETHYST (Quartz) The name comes from the Greek A-methystos, meaning 'not tipsy'. This powerful stone is connected with the third-eye chakra, and as such it is used on anything that relates to spiritual awareness, from aiding with meditation and tranquility, to attuning the bearer with the higher self and strengthening intuition and psychic power. It is also used to aid with prophetic dreams and divination. Other myths involving amethyst say it is a stone used to rid oneself of poisons. It carries a negative ion, which attacks poisonous positive ions, making the air around it more "breathable". It also aids in overcoming addiction, and it's been used since ancient times to guard oneself against drunkenness.

AVENTURINE GREEN (Quartz) This stone is considered to be a gambler's talisman as and is considered a "lucky" stone by many. Traditionally used to aid development of intuition, creativity, physical, emotional & intellectual flexibility. It's also thought to help promote growth, optimism, determination, prosperity, abundance, relaxation, recovery, enthusiasm and tolerance. Aventurine was revered by the ancient Tibetans. They used it to represent the "eyes" in sacred statues, thus symbolizing increased divinatory powers.

BLUE LACE AGATE: A beautiful graceful stone with blues and whites, lifting you up to unbelievable highs and giving you a feeling of wide open spaces and blue skies. It helps you reach a state of higher awareness and interact with spirits from the invisible worlds around us. A stone of awareness that facilitates reaching high spiritual places. Traditionally used to promote peace, patience inspiration, creativity and tranquility.

CARNELIAN: Stone of protection. Returns negativity to sender and helps protect against fear. Aids sociability, promotes confidence and positive thought. Is good for stabilizes all energies, spiritual, mental and physical.

Metaphysical Properties- Carnelian is one of those stones that should be in every healing kit. It is wonderful for working with the second chakra; creativity, reproduction and stability. Carnelian encourages curiosity and enthusiasm and is warm and energizing. Some like to use Carnelian to relieve their fear of death, while bringing an acceptance of the cycle of life. A good motivator in business, aids positive life choices, and dispels apathy.

CELESTITE: Also known as Celestine, it is thought to contain angelic or celestial properties. It offers a gentle but strong uplifting energy that will raise one's awareness and is considered to be an essential stone for connecting with spiritual realms or astral travel as well as aiding in dream recall. It is effective in strengthening psychic abilities, mental capacity for inspiration, creativity and discipline. Used to open the third eye to higher dimensions.

Note: Celestite is a soft stone that is easily scratched and its color fades if exposed to sunlight.

CITRINE: Stone of radiance. Instills an inner glow of love, confidence and happiness. Promotes mental and emotional clarity, lifting the spirit and soul creating alignment within you. Citrine is helpful for directing creative energy into the physical body. Some find it helpful in building self-esteem. This crystal is an invaluable aid to the digestion of all emotions.

Metaphysical Properties- Citrine has been called "the merchant stone." Assists in acquiring wealth and to maintain the state of wealth.

FLUORITE - Rainbow: Stabilizes and dispels chaotic stress in one's life. It can be used to increases perception and assist seeing the positive and negative of relationships. Clears air of psychic clutter.

GARNET: Stone of grounding and inner strength. Calms anger, assures love and faithfulness. Enhances internal fire, energy and vitality, imagination, self-esteem and will power.

Garnet can be used to remove negative energy from your chakras. It will assist one to balance the flow of energy around the body. You can also use this to help one to love themselves and others.

HEMATITE: This is a wonderful stone for preventing worry because it helps you to become more grounded (at ease). Hematite is also used for protection of oneself and their home. Some like to carry a small tumbled Hematite stone with them when they feel the need for protection from negative energy.

HOWLITE: A white gemstone with grey veins for good luck. Also calms, comforts and aids sleep. This stone inspires and helps achieve artistic projects & goals. Also stimulates imagination to draw new ventures and ideas into your life. Relieves stress, anger & pain, aids artistic endeavors/projects and helps contact your spirit guide.

MALACHITE: Absorbs energy, draws emotions to the surface, clears and activates the Chakras. An extremely powerful metaphysical stone, known as the "stone of transformation" and is used for deep energy cleaning.

Malachite amplifies energies of all kinds, both positive and negative. Said to be one of the most important healing stones, Malachite helps the user acknowledge, draw out, and discharge negative energy, including old emotional patterns, past traumas, and suppressed feelings.

MOONSTONE: Partially translucent with a milky sheen reminiscent of moonlight. Color shades include variations of earth tones: creams, peach, sand and pearly gray colors.

Moonstone is widely used for focusing on Lunar or feminine energies. Traditionally connected with promoting feminine health as well which makes it an important component of any medicine bag. A great stone for nurturing intuition and insight. Moonstone helps us to connect with all the different cycles we experience in life. Both men & women find Moonstone to be very soothing and use it to help relieve stress and aggression, bringing balance to the emotional body. Moonstone can also be used for good luck and safe traveling.

Working with the Third-Eye and Crown Chakras, Moonstone connects us to divine inspiration, and channels it into our own intuition. Working with Moonstone encourages introspection and judgment, yielding easier decision making. Moonstone also enhances one's emotional vision, bringing greater creative ability, and freedom of expression. These properties are also enhanced by Moonstone's ability to open one up to increased synchronicities, that we often cannot see due to our being wrapped up in our daily routines. Moonstone can also offer increased patience and allowing, so those newly found synchronicities can flow into our lives unimpeded.

MOSS AGATE: A beautiful stone with mottled, moss-like inclusion. It can aid in communication with nature spirits, natural energies and Gaia. Also used to help get into touch with earth and enhance plant growth.

PERIDOT was believed to be a stone of springtime by ancients who considered it a gift from Mother Nature. Peridot is a stone of lightness and beauty. Used in a necklace, peridot is a protector against negative emotions. In old Folk Lore Peridot was thought to have a healing effect on the gall bladder and liver.

PYRITE: Another highly protective stone, blocking or shielding you from negative energies of people, places and things. Some like to use Pyrite to stimulate the mind, recalling information when you need it the most. Good for those of us who can be forgetful.

Many people say Pyrite is good protection against illness. This high energy stone is good for a caregiver or healer during their work.

QUARTZ (CRYSTAL): Known for its healing abilities. It helps one to clear their mind and focus on what is needed. It helps to connect you to the physical plane with the universal plane energies. It is also considered a conductor of energy.

RAINBOW MOONSTONE: A stone overflowing with feminine wisdom and Goddess energy. It has a reflective calming energy, which helps to strengthen intuition, psychic perception and brings balance and harmony to all. The Rainbow effect invokes a spectrum of light, and helps bring a feeling of cleansing and uplifting energy. It has been said to have the power to help aid in granting wishes.

ROSE QUARTZ: One of the most popular metaphysical stones. Known as "The stone of unconditional love." Rose Quartz opens the heart to all forms of love and acceptance. Raises self-esteem and teaches one how to both give love to others and receive love to oneself. Rose Quartz eases guilt and balances emotions, lowering stress and bringing peace.

Known for its romantic properties. Rose Quartz can be used to attract love or to add trust and re-commitment to existing relationships. Helps bring passionate love back into being. Rose Quartz emits a calm, peaceful loving energy. May also help release unexpressed feelings about others.

The comforting and soothing energy of Rose Quartz can be used to balance the Heart Chakra and allows release of pent-up emotions and grief to help heal "emotional" wounds and soul trauma. It is often used to help heal a broken heart and aids in the power of forgiveness. Use Rose Quartz to bring calm and harmony during times of increased stress or crisis.

In old folk lore, Rose Quartz was used to encourage a beautiful complexion and thought to prevent wrinkles and help reduce weight.

SMOKEY QUARTZ: This stone works slowly and gently, while emitting high levels of energy. It is considered one of the more powerful metaphysical stones and is ideal for grounding, stabilizing and healing. Used to stimulate and purify the Root Chakra, and expanding consciousness into the physical body. Smokey Quartz is an essential part of any crystal collection, and is a must for the medicine bag.

SNOWFLAKE OBSIDIAN: Traditionally, snowflake obsidian is a stone of peace and tranquility. It helps to gently bring hidden imbalances to the surface, and may quietly reveal unhealthy patterns in your behavior that you might want to adjust. It can help you find balance in life, especially during times of change. Some use for spiritual protection, purifying, dissolves fear, shock, trauma, pain, tension and energy blocks. A beautiful Black stone with White patches or veins.

SODALITE: Said to promote companionship and can help form unity and fellowship within a group. Can also be used in group settings where cooperation is needed. Helps one speak openly and gain more confidence. Enhances communication and creative expression. Stimulates truthfulness and alleviates fear. May also prolong physical energy and endurance.

Sodalite is thought to help those encountering difficulties in their life, as it can bring unhealthy ingrained patterns to the surface to be released, revealing underlying causes to one's problems. Using Sodalite consistently by meditating with it or possibly sleeping with it under the pillow may help bring productive dreams. Sodalite is connected with the Throat and Third eye Chakras. Slightly sedative and is great for deepening meditation.

Folk Lore: Thought to aid both the metabolism, the immune system and is also believed to help regulate blood pressure and stabilize the thyroid.

SUNSTONE: This stone was associated with the Sun during the Renaissance because of its sparkling orange-gold hue. It was used by magicians to call upon the influences of the sun. It is a protective stone.

Symbolically, Sunstone is linked to Moonstone. Carry the two stones together to bring the influences of the Sun (Healing, Protection, and Success) into harmony with those of the Moon (Love, Peace, Spirituality). Placed before a white candle, Sunstone is thought to spread protective energies throughout your home.

TIGERS EYE - GOLDEN: Promotes balance, strength to get through difficult phases of life; relieves doubt and bestows decision making; vision and clarity. This stone has the properties of both the Earth and Sun. This can be used on the Solar Plexus Chakra to help open it. It is helpful with eye, throat and reproductive system disorders.

UNAKITE: Traditionally used to promote balance of the emotional body, higher spirituality. Allows us to release past burdens and move ahead with life.

You'll find several pages of additional lore on stones on the Gemstone & Crystal index page of our website.. There is also a wealth of information and IMAGES for a wide variety of stones in the Celtic Connection Magical Store. You can view this information at: http://wicca.com/stores/magical From the categories on the left, Click Crystals & Gemstones and then select Tumbled Stones.

For additional reading we recommend *Cunningham's Encyclopedia of Crystal, Gem and Metal Magic* and *101 Power Crystals* by Judy Hall. The second title has lots of great photos!

Using Herbs & Plants In Wiccan Ritual

The power of herbs and plants cannot be denied. Some have aromas that promote healing in our mind and spirit. Others contain oil that promote healing of our body when applied to our skin or consumed. Before all of the chemical based products came onto the market, our ancestors used plants and trees for many things. The leaves, bark, pulp and oils that came from them were used to create medicines, healing oils, perfumes, beauty creams and much more.

Learning about the energies in herbs or plants and how to use them can take years. If you want to master this subject you should plan on investing a lot of study time and reading countless books In this section, you will find a few helpful tips on how to collect and use herbs in your spells. I've included a glossary for you of the most common ones and their traditional uses.

When you gather flowers, herbs and plants for your rituals, pause for a minute to attune with them. They will be aiding you in your work and you should always thank them for their contribution.

Gently cut only what you need. It's a good practice to never take from a very young plant or cut more than twenty-five percent of a plant's growth. If you need a limb or bark from a tree, try to find a fallen branch and use what the tree has already given.

Many Wiccans like to leave a thank you gift at the base of the plant or tree. A coin, a bit of food, a small crystal or stone may be used for this purpose. Cover the offering and you are done.

In your spells you will often be using plants for their aroma. At other times they may simply be representative of the season's bounty. We don't recommended Ingesting herbs in your rituals unless you are familiar with their energies and how they react.

A Witches' Herbal Reference Guide

Courtesy of The Celtic Connection
http://wicca.com

In this section you will find a reasonably comprehensive list of herbs for both magical and healing/health uses. While not complete, it will give you a good base of knowledge to start from.

ALOE
Magical attributes: Beauty, protection, success, peace.
Uses: Aloe has always been known for its healing qualities. Great for treating wounds and maintaining healthy skin. It may be applied right from the plant or in gel form for burns, sunburns, and can relieve poison ivy rash and helps to combat a variety of bacteria that commonly cause infections in skin wounds. It is also an excellent additive for soaps and creams as a conditioner.
After using gel from a leaf the opened leaf will seal itself so you can store it in a sealed plastic bag in the refrigerator for future uses.

ANGELICA
Magical attributes: Protection, Exorcism.
Uses: Grow in the garden as a protection. Carry the root with you as an amulet. Burn the dried leaves in exorcism rituals.

ANISE
Magical attributes: Protection, purification, awareness, joy.
Uses: For treating coughs, bronchitis and a stuffy nose, it loosens bronchial congestion, making it easier to cough it up and expel it. A good breath freshener in the morning, and if kept by the bed it will prevent bad dreams. Also a digestive aid and can relieve an upset stomach and flatulence when taken as a tea, and a treatment for colic. Also suggested that anise may be beneficial to women because certain chemicals in the plant are chemical cousins to the female hormone estrogen. Though it is mild, anise may help to relieve the discomfort of menopause. In traditional folk medicine it

has been used to promote milk production in nursing mothers. Its recommended dosage would be 1 teaspoonful of seeds for every cup of boiling water, steep 10-20 minutes and strain, drink 3 cups a day for maximum effect. A good general cleansing bath is made with a handful of anise seeds and a few bay leaves. A pillow of anise keeps away nightmares. Also a good sedative.

APPLE
Magical attributes: Love spells, good luck.

ASH
Magical attributes: A tree with protective qualities, it is used to make brooms for purification and wands for healing. The leaves placed beneath a pillow induce psychic dreams. The leaves bring luck and good fortune when carried in a pocket of bag worn around the neck.

BALM of GILEAD
Magical attributes: The buds are carried to ease a broken heart and can be added to love and protection charms and spells.

BASIL
Magical attributes: Protection, love, wealth (if carried in your wallet), healing relationships, ensuring faithfulness in a mate, courage, fertility, exorcism.
Uses: It is good as a tea for calming the nerves, settling the stomach, and easing cramps and good for the bladder. In tincture form, also makes a good hair rinse for brunettes. An ingredient of the Purification bath sachet. Add to love sachets and incenses.

BAY LAUREL
Magical attributes: wisdom, protection, psychic powers, banishes negative energy.
Uses: DO NOT TAKE INTERNALLY-use as a poultice on chest for bronchitis and chest colds.

BAY LEAVES
Magical attributes: Psychic visions and dreams, repels negativity and evil.

BENZOIN
Magical attributes: Used widely in purification incenses. Tincture of benzoin preserves oils and preparations.

BETONY
Magical attributes: Add to incenses of protection and purification. Sleep on a pillow stuffed with betony to prevent nightmares.

CARAWAY
Magical attributes: Protection, Passion
Uses: Add to love sachets and charms to attract a lover in the more physical aspect. Also a mild stimulant for digestion.

CARNATION
Magical attributes: Worn by witches for protection during the "Burning Times", adds energy and power when used during a ritual as an incense.

CATNIP
Magical attributes: Cat magic, familiars, joy, friendship, love.
Uses: Its flowers and leaves have often been used to treat colds and insomnia. It lowers fevers, dries up post nasal drip, gets rid of bad headaches and relieves sore aching bones due to colds and flus, when taken in tea form, 2-3 times daily. As incense it may be used to consecrate magical tools.

CAMOMILE
Magical attributes: Good as a meditation incense, for centering, peace, sprinkle in your home for protection, healing, money.
Uses: Is an excellent herb both internally and externally for calming. Great for digestion, fevers, burns, is anti-inflammatory for wounds, acts as a sedative for nervous disorders, and relieves

stomachaches and diarrhea in infants and small children (always using in diluted form). In tea form, made of 2 teaspoons of the herb steeped for 5 minutes in a cup of boiling water is a gentle sleep inducer. Chamomile also makes an excellent insect repellent, simply splash some tea on face arms and feet. It is also a good hair rinse for blondes. Plant chamomile in your garden to be the guardian of the land, and you will have certain success.

CARAWAY
Magical attributes: Used in love charms to attract a lover.
Uses: Culinary herb.

CELANDINE
Magical attributes: Helps the wearer escape unfair imprisonment and entrapment, cures depression.

CINNAMON
Magical attributes: Spiritual quests, augmenting power, love, success, psychic work, healing, cleansing. Used in incenses for healing, clairvoyance, high spiritual vibrations. Reputed to be a male aphrodisiac. Use in prosperity charms.
Uses: It is recommended as a skin astringent and digestive aid in tea form. Ground, or taken with milk, good balance after a heavy meal or dessert. Also used for diarrhea, dysentery or general indigestion. It is an excellent aromatic and makes a good anointing oil for any magical working.

CLOVER
Magical attributes: Associated with the Triple Goddess. Use in rituals for beauty, youth, healing injuries, curing madness. A Four-leaved clover enables one to see fairies, and as a general good-luck charm.

CLOVE
Magical attributes: Wear in an amulet or charm to dispel negativity and bind those who speak ill of you. Cloves strung on a red thread

can be worn as a protective charm. Money matters, visions, cleansing and purification.

Uses: It has a mild antiseptic quality for toothaches (chew), or in tea form it is an expectorant for colds, also good foe nausea or vomiting. It is an antibacterial, antiseptic, and analgesic, which means it helps prevent disease and infection.

COMFREY

Magical attributes: Safe travel spells, money, healing, honoring the Crone aspect of the Goddess.

Uses: Has been known to slow bleeding, aid colds, ease burns. As a poultice or a tea, comfrey may be applied to bites, sores, rashes, broken bones, and cuts. Also a good ingredient for lotions to soothe sunburn.

CORIANDER

Magical attributes: Protection of home and serenity, peace, good in ritual drinks, incenses for longevity and love spells.

Uses: If added to wine, it makes a good love potion for 2 consenting parties. To use in this fashion, grind 7 grains of coriander and mix into a wine and drink. Also used in love sachets and charms.

COWSLIP

Magical uses: Luck in love, a woman who washes her face with milk infused with cowslip will draw her beloved closer to her. Induces contact with departed loved ones during dreams.

CYPRESS

Magical uses: Connected to death in all of its aspects. The smoke of Cypress can be used to consecrate ritual objects.

DAISY

Magical uses: Decorate the house with daisies at Midsummer's Eve to bring happiness to the home and to obtain the blessings of faeries. Daisies are also worn at Midsummer for luck and blessings.

In the old times, young maidens would weave and wear daisy chains in their hair to attract their beloved.

DANDELION
Magical attributes: Divination, welcoming, messages.
Uses: The ground root can act as a coffee substitute, and the flowers make a lovely wine. A superb cleansing tonic and the milky juice is a diuretic, a tonic and a relief for common stomach problems. Use a handful of flower tops to 1 pint of boiling water, steep 10 minutes and strain. Drink this several times a day. Use the milky latex from the stem, rub on a wart several times daily and soon it's gone. Also good for night blindness.

DILL
Magical attributes: Useful in love charms. May also be hung in children's rooms to protect them from bad dreams.
Uses: A culinary herb.

DRAGONS BLOOD
Magical uses: Widely used in love, protection and purification spells. Keep a piece under the bed to cure impotency. Carried for good luck. May be dissolved in the bath for strong purification.

ELECAMPANE
Magical uses: Useful in raising spirits and to aid in meditation.

ELDER
Magical uses: Branches are widely used for wands. One must always be cautious to ask permission from the Elder Dryad before cutting or harvesting Elder limbs or leaves and berries to avoid very bad luck. It is also considered very bad luck to burn Elder wood. The leaves hung around the doors and windows will ward off evil.

EUCALYPTUS
Magical uses: Used in healing rituals, charms and amulets. Place the leaves around a blue candle and burn for healing energies. Green

pods worn around the neck ease the discomfort of colds, sore throats and congestion.

EYEBRIGHT
Magical uses: Anoint eyelids with the infusion daily to induce clairvoyant visions and psychic dreams.

FENNEL
Magical attributes: Purification, protection, healing, money.
Uses: Sometimes employed as an appetite suppressant and digestive aid. Used in tea form to expel mucus. Chew the seeds slowly for really bad breath, or use the fluid extract to rub on gums.

FERN
Magical uses: The Fern is an extremely powerful protective plant. Grow them in and around the house for protection from evil and negativity.

FRANKINCENSE
Magical uses: A very powerful aid to meditation. Use to purify ritual spaces and invoke a spiritual frame of mind.

GARDENIA
Magical uses: Used to attract true love.

GARLIC
Magical uses: A very protective herb, healing, good weather, courage, exorcism.
Uses: A culinary herb.

GINGER
Magical attributes: Power, success, love, money matters.
Uses: Acts as an aid to ingestion or colds (tea form). Also in tea form, good for cramps, to stimulate the digestive organs, migraines and nausea, external stiffness. Can be added to the bath as a way to ease pain and increase circulation, but only use a few sprinkles,

not too much, like cayenne, ginger quickly brings the blood to the surface of the skin. For pain you can also soak cloths in ginger tea and apply them directly to the painful areas. Add in cooking to detoxify meat, especially chicken. A good healing tea is made from a pinch of peppermint, a pinch of ginger and either a pinch of clove powder or 2 bruised cloves, add 1 cup of hot water and steep.

GINSENG
Magical attributes: Love, wishes, beauty, desire.
Uses: Stimulant, tonic, and agent for prolonged life. Also a mild pain killer, and improves blood circulation. Reported to successfully treat asthma, bronchitis, cancer, flatulence, diabetes, weakness, fever, coughs and heartburn, and a mild stimulant. In tea form it helps to relieve stress and moderate heart disease.

GARLIC
Magical attributes: Protection, healing, good weather, courage, exorcism.
Uses: Lowers tension, eases colds, and improves circulation. Garlic vinegar can be used to disinfect wounds and soothe rheumatic pain and any common pain (made from one liter of vinegar and ten cloves of crushed garlic steeped for at least 10 days). Shrinks warts, relieves pain from teeth and earaches. Good for high and low blood pressure and removing parasites and infections. To ease the pain of aching joints, a toothache or an earache, place a crushed raw bulb of garlic on a piece of gauze and place over the area of pain. For joints, try using garlic paste.

HAWTHORN
Magical uses: Used in protective sachets and amulets against evil influences. Promotes happiness in marriage or a relationship. It is bad luck to cut down a hawthorn. Burn the berries as incense when you need energy and change in life.

HAZEL

Magical uses: Hazel wood is excellent for an all-purpose wand. Forked branches can be used for divining. Sprigs of Hazel can be carried for good luck; they are especially powerful if bound together by red and gold thread.

HENBANE

Magical uses: Carried to attract the love of a woman. Was once used as an ingredient in a Witches flying ointment. Henbane is extremely poisonous and the upmost caution is urged.

HIGH JOHN the CONQUEROR ROOT

Magical uses: Use this as an additive to candle anointing oils, and charms to increase their strength.

HOLLY

Magical uses: Planted around the home for protection against evil. The leaves and berries can be carried by a man to heighten his masculinity, virility and to attract a lover.

HONEYSUCKLE

Magical uses: Used widely in prosperity spells and love charms.

HOPS

Magical uses: Used in healing incenses and charms. A mild sedative. Hops placed in a pillow will help with sleep.

HYSSOP

Magical uses: Use in purification baths, protective and banishing spells. Hyssop was widely used during the Middle Ages for purification, cleansing and consecration rituals. If burnt as incense or thrown into a fire it is said one may draw upon magical dragon energy.

IVY

Magical uses: Protects the houses it grows around and over from evil and harm. In the old traditions, Ivy and Holly were given to newlyweds as good-luck charms.

JASMINE

Magical uses: Used in love spells, charms and sachets. Women have used Jasmine from the earliest recorded history because of its seductive effects on men.

JUNIPER

G/P/E: Masculine, Sun, Fire.

Magical uses: Protection against accidents, harm and theft. The berries are used to attract lovers once dried and worn as a charm.

LAVENDER

Magical attributes: Sleep, long life, peace, wishes, protection, love, purification, visions, attracting men, clarity of thought.

Uses: Has strong antiseptic qualities. Mild infusions (3 tablespoons to 6 cups of water) make a good sedative, headache treatment, and digestive aid. Used in oil or tincture form to heal cuts, burns or scalds, bites. This also acts as a tonic and may be used for colds, chills, and the flu. Lavender is an excellent aromatic, usually mixing well with other floral scents. An ingredient in the Purification bath sachet, also used in purification incenses. It is thrown onto the Midsummer fires by Witches as a sacrifice to the ancient gods. Lavender is a frequent addition to healing sachets, especially bath mixtures, and is added to incense to cause sleep. Lavender is a great antibiotic, antidepressant, sedative and detoxify. Stimulates the immune system.

LEMON

Magical attributes: Purification, love, blessings.

Uses: Sweetens breath. Antiseptic, antibacterial and hypotensive. For chills and sore throat, the juice of a lemon mixed in a glass of honey and warm water, taken 3 times daily should help. For nose bleeds, apply a small piece of cotton, soaked in lemon juice. In oil form it is used for treating warts, insect bites, tension headaches, eliminates cellulite, and is an anti-wrinkle tonic. Stimulates the digestive system. Also makes a good skin cleanser, hair rinse for blondes, and cleaning agent for brass and silver.

LEMON BALM
Magical uses: Love potions, aphrodisiacs, fertility anti-depressant. Drink as an infusion to soothe emotional pains after a relationship ends.

LEMON VERBENA
Magical uses: Love charms, youth, beauty and attractiveness to the opposite sex. Wear around your neck or place under a pillow to prevent dreams.

LILAC
Magical attributes: Protection, warding off evil or banishing rituals, beauty, love, harmony and balance.

LINDEN
Magical uses: Associated with conjugal love or attraction and longevity.

LOVAGE
Magical uses: Add the dried and powdered root to cleansing and purification baths to release negativity. Carry to attract love and the attention of the opposite sex.

MANDRAKE
Magical uses: A protective charm for the home. The root was believed to increase fertility in women and impotency in men when carried. To charge a mandrake root with your personal energy, sleep with it for three nights prior to the full moon. The root can be carried to increase courage.

MARIGOLD

Magical attributes: Prophesy, legal matters, the psychic, seeing magical creatures, love, clairvoyance, dreams, business or legal affairs and renewing personal energy.

Uses: For internal use the flowers are prepared by infusion and recommended for the flu, fever, rheumatism, jaundice, and painful menstruation. Externally, buds are made into compresses for the treatment of burns. Marigold petal ointment can help chapped hands and varicose veins, also works wonders with eczema and inflammation. To ease inflammation, dip a compress into a strong marigold tea combined with an equal part of apple cider vinegar. Sprains can also be helped with marigold petals steeped in vinegar, or make a lotion with milk. Simmer 12 heads in 2 cups milk, steep, strain and apply. Also use as an antiseptic in first aid. Place the flower beneath the head at night to induce clairvoyant dreams. Sometimes added to love sachets. It should be gathered at noon.

MARJORAM

Magical attributes: protection, love, healing.

Uses: Add to all love charms or place a piece in rooms for protection. Give to a grieving person to bring them happiness.

MEADOWSWEET

Magical uses: Protection against evil influences, promotes love, balance and harmony. A sacred herb of the Druids. Place meadowsweet on the altar when making love charms and conducting love spells to increase their potency. Wear at Lammas to join with the Goddess.

MINT (SPEARMINT & PEPPERMINT)

Magical attributes: Money, healing, strength, augment power, luck, travel.

Uses: Mint in tea form aids upset stomachs, flu, and can be used to ease hiccups. Inhalations of the leaves in boiling water are recommended for head colds and asthma. Mint tea used instead of aspirin is great for headaches, particularly premenstrual headaches. Nervous headaches can be relieved if you lie in a dark room with fresh peppermint leaves on the forehead. Aids the respiratory and circulatory systems. An anti-inflammatory and an antiseptic. Ideal for treating indigestion, flatulence, varicose veins, headaches, migraines, skin irritations, rheumatism, toothache, and general fatigue.

MISTLETOE
Magical uses: Worn for protection and to attract love, or to help conceive.

MUGWORT
Magical uses: Clairvoyance, psychic dreams, astral projection, protection. Place in the shoes for protection and to prevent fatigue on long journeys. The fresh leaves rubbed on a magick mirror or crystal ball will strengthen divinatory abilities. Mugwort is perhaps the most widely used Witches herb of all time.

MULLEIN
Magical uses: Courage, protection from wild animals, protection from evil spirits, cleansing of ritual and psychic places before and after working there. Also used for cleansing and purifying ritual tools and altars.

MYRRH
Magical uses: Purifying and protective incense for ritual areas. Can be used to consecrate tools.
Uses: Excellent insect repellent and as a tincture it is good for bad breath and gum problems.

MYRTLE
Magical uses: Myrtle was sacred to the Greek Goddess Venus and has been used in love charms and spells throughout history. Grow indoors for good luck. Carry or wear Myrtle leaves to attract love; charms made of the wood have special magickal properties. Wear

fresh Myrtle leaves while making love charms, potions or during rituals for love.

NETTLE
Magical attributes: To advert danger, protection, healing, courage, antidote for many poisons.
Uses: Use gloves to handle so as to avoid getting pricked. High in vitamin C and iron and when in tea form can ease asthma and increase your energy levels.

NUTMEG
Magical uses: Clairvoyance and psychic power of visions.

OAK
Magical uses: The Oak is a sacred tree in many cultures. A Witch will often seek out a grove of Oak to perform rites. It has always been considered unlucky to cut down an oak. After getting permission from the tree's Dryad, burn oak leaves for purification of ritual spaces. Oak is often used for all-purpose wands and they imbue great power. The acorns have been carried to increase fertility in women and to increase sexual appeal by men, preserve youth and to banish illness. Hang Oak over windows and doors to protect your house from evil spirits.

ONION
Magical uses: Protection and healing. Place cut onions in a sick person's room to absorb the illness. Leave them overnight and throw away in the morning.

ORANGE
Magical uses: The dried and powdered peel is added to love and fertility charms.

ORRIS ROOT
Magical uses: Love, sexual appeal. Use in charms, amulets, sachets, incenses and baths.

PARSLEY

Magical attributes: Fresh parsley leaves in tea form are a treatment for cramps, while dried root decoctions eases urinary infections and arthritis. Externally, crushed leaves relieve insect bites, and may be applied in poultice form to sprains.

Uses: Widely used as a culinary herb

PATCHOULI

Magical uses: Aphrodisiac and attractant of lovers for either sex

.

PENNYROYAL

Magical uses: Protection, weariness, deters insects. Avoid Pennyroyal while pregnant.

BLACK PEPPER

Magical uses: Use in protective charms.

PERIWINKLE

Magical uses: Protection against evil influences. Hang around doors and windows.

PIMPERNEL

Magical uses: Wear to detect falsehood to prevent or know when others are lying to you.

PINE

Magical attributes: Attunement to nature, centering, cleansing, healing, productivity, purification against illness, a good winter incense, fertility charms.

Uses: Pine buds prepared by decoction act as an expectorant and antiseptic. This same mixture can be used for inhalation for head colds, although it is easier to toss some needles in hot water. Green cones and needles can be added to bath water to ease muscle pains and swelling. For magic, pine is best suited for its aromatic qualities of bringing one back into balance, and enhancing connection with the natural world.

POPPY
Magical uses: Eat poppy seeds as a fertility charm, just don't take a urine test at work for a few days afterward. Carry the seeds or dried seed-pod as a prosperity charm.

ROSE
Magical attributes: Love, friendship, luck, protection, psychic power and divination.
Uses: Conserves of roses or rose petals in honey are often recommended for nausea and sore throats. Roses are high in vitamin C.

ROSEMARY
Magical attributes: Improve memory, sleep, purification, youth, love, power, healing, protection, intellectual.
Uses: Promotes healing of wounds, acts as an antiseptic, and can be a mild stimulant. Good in teas for treating flu, stress, and headaches or body aches. Mental and physical booster. Used for treating (oil form) muscular sprains, arthritis, rheumatism, depression, fatigue, memory loss, migraine headaches, coughs, flu and diabetes. Excellent remedy for acne or cellulite. When the leaves are soaked in wine for two weeks, small glasses may be taken as a digestive aid. Oil of rosemary is excellent in hair conditioners, and the flowers of this herb may be added to lotion recipes to improve the complexion. Add to all purification bath sachets, love incenses, and protection incenses. Make a simple of rosemary and use it to cleanse the hands before working magic, if you have no time for a regular ritual bath. Burn rosemary and juniper as a healing and recuperation incense.

ROWAN
Magical uses: Protection, good luck, healing.

RUE
Magical uses: Protection, preventing illness, clearness of mind, purification of ritual spaces and tools, clearing the mind of emotional clutter.

THYME
Magical attributes: Sleep, psychic energy, courage, healing, purification incense, magickal cleansing baths, a renewing of one's personal energy, warding off of negative energy.
Uses: Powerful antibacterial, antibiotic, and diuretic properties. It helps eliminate wastes from the body. It is used in treating whooping coughs, warts, rheumatism and acne. A strong antiseptic which when prepared by infusion is useful for poor digestion, exhaustion, colds, and infections, and with honey is an effective treatment for sore throats. Also used in tea form as a fever breaker, headache reducer and to be rid of intestinal worms, and can be used as a mouthwash. Also, a great insect repellent. Use both the leaves and flowers. This tea works best for headaches when taken cold. Take a magical cleansing bath in the spring of thyme and marjoram (used in tea form or whole herbs). A pillow stuffed with it cures nightmares.

TUMERIC
Uses: added to warm milk it regulates menstrual cycle.

VALERIAN
Magical attributes: Love, calming, sleep, purification or relaxing baths.
Uses: Use the dried, powdered root. Promotes relaxation while counteracting the effects of insomnia, anxiety, nervousness, headaches, premenstrual syndrome and menstrual cramping. For sleep, before bed take 1 teaspoon of herb to 1 pint of water and simmer. Also acts as a good substitute for catnip. Use the fresh herb in spells of love, also to get fighting couples together. Used in the Purification bath sachet.

VANILLA

Magical uses: The bean is used in a love charms, the oil is worn as an aphrodisiac.

VERVAIN

Magical uses: Ritual cleansing or sacred space, magical cleansing baths, purification incenses. Hang over the bed to prevent nightmares. Love and protection charms, Vervain is also an excellent for use in prosperity charms and spells as it brings good luck and inspiration.

VIOLET

Magical uses: Mix with lavender for a powerful love charm. A Violet and Lavender compress will aid in eliminating headaches. The flowers are carried as a good-luck charm. The scent will soothe, clear the mind and relax the wearer.

WALNUT

Magical uses: Carry the nut as a charm to promote fertility and strengthen the heart.

WILLOW

Magical uses: Willow wands can be used for healing. The Willow will bring the blessings of the Moon upon those who plant it or have it on their property. Willows can be used to bind together witch's brooms and a forked willow branch is widely used in water witching and dowsing.

WITCH HAZEL

Magical attributes: Protection, chastity, healing the heart.
Uses: In tincture form it is good as a mouth rinse and to ease hemorrhoids. As a compress, witch hazel can be applied to insect bites and other skin irritations.

WORMWOOD

Magical uses: Wormwood is burned to gain protection from wandering spirits. Used in divinatory and clairvoyance incenses, initiation rites and tests of courage. Enables the dead to be released from this plane so they may find peace.

YARROW

Magical uses: Courage, love, marriage charms, dispelling negativity, psychic abilities, divination.

Uses: A very potent healer, it intensifies the medicinal action of other herbs taken with it. Helps eliminate toxins (good for colds). Most useful in its abilities to staunch blood flow. In poultice form, it is useful against infections and swelling. In magic there is evidence that yarrow was often used as a component in incantations. The tea drunk prior to divination will enhance one's powers of perception (a touch of peppermint brightens this brew up and always works better). Also drink the tea to stop arthritis symptoms such as swelling and inflammation associated with weather divination and generally end all aching, sore muscles, or stiff joints or back pain. A powerful incense additive for divination and love spells.

For additional reading about the magical use of herbs we highly recommend *Cunningham's Encyclopedia of Magical Herbs* and *Magical Herbalism*. Both books are written by Scott Cunningham.

Part 2: Talking to the Goddess

When we learn to connect with Mother Earth and show our deep respect for nature, we draw closer to the Divine and open our lives to many blessings. In this book, you'll read excerpts from some ancient texts that reveal how our ancestors communicated with the Divine through nature.

These ancient texts were also referred to as the Secret Teachings or the Teachings of the Elect. While they are not traditionally used to teach Wicca, they parallel many Pagan traditions and beliefs that have been passed down through the centuries. These writings helped me gain a deeper understanding of the Old Ways and the nature-based beliefs that are still being taught today. It is my hope that they will do the same for you.

In Talking to the Goddess, you'll explore how the five elements of Earth, Air, Fire, Water and Spirit can improve your ability to communicate with the Divine. These elements have been honored in rituals for centuries. However, in the ancient Essene texts they were also known as the Earthly Mother's "messengers". Communing with them daily was believed to strengthen your body, mind and spirit and draw you closer to the Divine.

The elements can be a complicated topic. There are many ways to honor and work with them. **However, for the purpose of this book we are only going to explore how they affect our communication with the Goddess.** For additional reading on working with the elements, I highly recommend *Wicca Elemental Magic* by Lisa Chamberlain.

A chapter has been dedicated to each of the five elements and how they help connect you with the Divine. You'll then read a little about communicating with plants and animals. Finally, you'll explore common divination tools and meditation techniques you can use when you need a little extra guidance. Once you've opened all your lines of communication, you'll discover just how easy it is to talk to the Goddess on a daily basis.

Connecting With The Goddess

In this modern age, we can communicate with most of our friends and family instantly. We relay messages by phone, text or Internet posts and in most cases, a response is immediate. Easy, fast and clear communication is what we expect today, no matter what part of the world we are trying to connect with.

The Goddess is not a world away from us. Most agree that the Divine is WITHIN us and can be found in everything around us as well. So why then, do so many feel disconnected from a force that resides within them?

When life gets challenging and we face financial, health or relationship problems, it can feel like the Divine has abandoned us. We often think that the Goddess is just not listening to us, but in reality, we are usually the one not listening. In most cases, simply repairing or clearing our communication lines to the Divine makes all the difference!

We all understand that packing a cell phone around with us does not guarantee that our family and friends can always reach us. Our battery must be charged and we need to have our phone turned on. Likewise, we would not expect to get an email from anyone if we had no established Internet connection. If you want the Goddess to be able to talk to you, you'll need to make sure you provide her with clear working lines of communication.

That's where the elements come in. Communing with Earth, Air, Fire, Water and Spirit can open your lines of communication and strengthen your connection with the Divine! Each of the next five chapters will cover one of the elements and some of the ways that particular element can help connect you to the Goddess.

Knowing how to talk to the Goddess and her elemental "messengers" can make a huge difference in your relationship with her. The Goddess loves to send "signs" to help us find our way, but we need to recognize those signs and understand what she is trying to communicate to us. In Talking to the Goddess, you'll discover how to open your lines of communication so you'll always hear her voice and recognize the messages she sends your way.

In his book *Earth Power*, Scott Cunningham was talking about the elements when he wrote *"Attuning and working with these energies in magic not only lends you the power to affect dramatic changes in your life, it also allows you to sense your own place in the larger scheme of Nature."*

Please note that working with the Goddess and her elemental energies should not be something that you only do on specific days or during rituals. Communing with the Divine daily can change your life dramatically. The Goddess is always listening and always responding to every thought and feeling you send out. Just because you may not be thinking about her, does not mean that she is not responding to everything you think and do.

The next chapter will explore how the element of Earth can improve communication with the Divine.

Your Body And Mother EARTH

Blessed is the Child of Light who is strong in body, for he shall have oneness with the Earth. Thou shalt celebrate a daily feast with all the gifts of the Messenger of Earth: The golden wheat and corn, the purple grapes of autumn, the ripe fruits of the trees, the amber honey of the bees.

The earth has always represented abundance, strength and stability. In rituals an object may be buried in the ground as an offering, or to allow its energies to disperse and be absorbed by Mother Earth. But by far, the Earth's greatest gift to us, is the gift of good health. We plant tiny seeds in her rich soil and are rewarded with foods that nourish our body.

In the ancient texts of the Essenes, they shared their belief that eating "living" or unprocessed foods would insure a long and healthy life, while eating processed or "dead" foods would separate them from the Divine and lead to an early death. If you wanted to be part of their group and learn the Teachings of the Elect, you were required to eat only from the table of the Earthly Mother.

"The Earthly Mother and I are one. Never will I desert her and always will she nourish and sustain my body. You will feel the power of the Earthly Mother flowing through your body like the river when it is swollen with rains and courses mightily with a great noise."

While I can't say I have felt the energy of a raging river within me after a meal, I clearly feel much more energetic when I eat fresh fruits and vegetables, than I do after a meal of cooked or processed foods. If I am planning an activity that requires energy or focused concentration, I grab a piece of fresh fruit. Try eating only from the table of your Earthly Mother when you want to boost your energy or sharpen your mind and see what happens.

"First shall the Son of Man seek peace with his own body. For his body is as a mountain pond that reflects the sun when it is still and clear; but when it is full of mud and stones it reflects nothing."

If you look into a muddy pond, little will be revealed to you and if your body is full of sludge or processed foods, you will have a much harder time receiving messages from the Goddess. For centuries, many spiritual leaders have believed that eating a diet of fresh fruits and vegetables was essential to strengthening their connection with the Divine.

Today most belief systems do not give much guidance on what you should or should not eat. With a few exceptions, you are free to indulge in what you enjoy. But keep in mind that the fuel you put in your body will affect your physical, mental AND spiritual function. This is because the body mind and spirit work as one. You need to be in good health physically if you want maximum clarity of mind and a strong spiritual connection with the Goddess.

Most of us draw from her energy by walking barefoot through her soft green grass or sitting quietly on the ground in the shade of an old tree. But she will also bless you with increased energy and a stronger mind and spirit if you eat her gifts of fresh produce. So as you honor the element of Earth and her power to grow vibrant, healthy plants from tiny seeds, know also that she has the power to make you more vibrant and healthy as well.

But eating from the table of your Earthly Mother is not the only way to improve your lines of communication with the Divine. The element of Air offers you gifts that may be even more powerful in helping you connect with the Goddess and they are totally free!

Your Health And AIR

"Messenger of Air, Holy messenger of the Earthly Mother, enter deep within me, as the swallow plummets from the sky, that I may know the secrets of the wind and the music of the stars."

*"Breathe long and deeply, that the messenger of Air may be brought within you. **For the rhythm of thy breath is the key of knowledge** which doth reveal the Holy Law."*

When we list the things that are most important to us, virtually no one includes air. We take it for granted, even though we need it to live and the quality of our air has a significant impact on our mental and physical health.

Air is an element through which you receive information about the world around you. If you're doing a working related to communication, wisdom or the powers of the mind, Air is the element to focus on.

In many rituals, it is represented by aromatherapy or music. Adding incense, oils, music or nature sounds to your spells and rituals can help you create an "air" of magic and put you in the right frame of mind to talk to the Goddess. As the scents and sounds are carried through the air, they transform the space around you and influence your thoughts and feelings.

While these traditions can help set the proper atmosphere, there is another activity that may be even more beneficial in opening the lines of communication with the Goddess.

Many traditions use breath as a tool for disciplining the body and accessing the inner spirit. When you begin to do breathwork, you may find you have greater recall of dreams and easier access to altered states of consciousness. Focused breathing has been used for centuries to help connect the conscious and unconscious mind.

It also plays a key role in communication with the Goddess. Actually, it is the breath or spirit with in us that connects us to every living thing. The English word "spirit" comes from the Latin word "spiritus" or breath. The Hebrew word "ruach" and the Greek word "pneuma" are also translated as both spirit and breath. In many traditions the breath and spirit are the same.

Just as you use physical exercise to strengthen your body, you can use breathing techniques to exercise your spirit. Strengthening your spirit is a wonderful way to improve your lines of communication with the Goddess.

Your breathing represents the movement of spirit. And it can be a primary means of raising spiritual awareness.

You always want to make sure you are free of stress and negative energy before talking to the Divine. When deep breathing is used before rituals or magic, it can help you relax and ensure you are sending forth the right message to the Divine.

Controlled breathing should fill you with peace and improve your overall well-being. Breathe deeply to get rid of the day's stress. As you exhale, let the stress go and inhale peace. Filling your lungs with the element of Air helps to increase blood flow to the brain and this will boost your concentration and visualization efforts, making it easier to talk to the Goddess.

"In the midst of the fresh air of the forest and fields, there shalt thou find the messenger of Air. Patiently she waits for thee to leave the dank and crowded holes of the city. Seek her then and draw deeply of the healing draught which she doth offer thee."

In the passage above, it is clear the Essenes knew fresh Air could heighten the senses. If possible, practice deep breathing in a forest or field, far from the polluted air of our cities. When you breathe deeply of the air in Mother Earth's natural surroundings, you'll experience the greatest peace and health benefits.

Deep breathing can be done in any position that is comfortable for you. Sit or lie down and relax your body. Slowly inhale through your nose to a count of three, four or five, whatever is most comfortable for you. Pause momentarily, then exhale to the same slow count. Repeat this several times, gradually slowing your breath rate. Do not hold your breath past the level of comfort. The inhalation, retaining and exhalation should be controlled, calm and free of tension.

As you inhale, breathe in peace, love, health and tranquil thoughts, then breathe out any stress, hate, anger or illness you feel within.

"We worship the Holy Breath which is placed higher than all the other things created. For lo, the eternal and sovereign luminous space where rule the unnumbered stars, is the air we breathe in and the air we breathe out."

And in the moment betwixt the breathing in and the breathing out, is hidden all the mysteries of the Infinite Garden.

Breathwork is often used in yoga and meditation exercises. It is a powerful approach to self-exploration and healing. Because it is so important, meditation was given its own chapter at the end of this book. There you'll read about several other breathing techniques that can help you relax and raise your awareness. But first, it's time to explore how the element of Fire can improve your communication with the Goddess!

Your Energy And FIRE

"Messenger of the Sun! There is no warmth without thee, no fire without thee, no life without thee. Green leaves of the trees do worship thee and through thee the tiny wheat kernel become a river of golden grass moving with the wind. Through thee is opened the flower in the center of my body. Therefore will I never hide myself from thee. messenger of Sun. Holy messenger of the Earthly Mother, enter the holy temple within me and give me the Fire of Life!"

In many ancient traditions, the element of Fire was viewed as a masculine energy. The Sun represented the God and the Earth was the Goddess or feminine aspect of the Divine. In folklore the masculine Sun would cover the feminine Earth and life would be renewed each year. Candles or fires were often lit in rituals and celebrations to honor the power and cycles of the Sun.

But how can the element of Sun possibly help us communicate with the Goddess? It all comes back to our health. When we don't get enough exposure to the sun, our bodies become low in vitamin D. Low vitamin D blood levels are linked to many health issues, including a higher risk of cognitive impairment or brain fog. This has been confirmed in many studies.

"...And you will feel the rays of the rising sun enter into the center point of your body. There in the center where the messengers of day and of night mingle, the power of the sun shall be yours to direct to any part of your body, for the messengers dwell therein."

You may not get enough sunlight if you spend a lot of time inside or use sunscreen. It's also difficult to get enough vitamin D from the sun during the winter. Vitamin D supplements can be helpful when you just can't get outside, but they will not be as beneficial as the real thing.

Communing with the element of Sun for just a few minutes each day can help rid the body of toxins and reduce the risk of diseases that affect the brain. It can also help regulate the immune system and enhance nerve conduction or signals to your brain.

In the Teachings of the Elect manuscript, we are told that the messenger of the Sun can bless us with good health. However like fire, too much sun can be destructive, so don't overdo it.

"Messenger of Sun! Dart forth thy rays upon me! Let them touch me; let them penetrate me! I give myself to thee and thy embrace, Bless me with the fire of life!"

Your Emotions And WATER

"And it shall be for healing, for the power of the messenger of Water is very great, and when you speak to her, she will send her power wherever you command."

Water has always been used for healing or purification purposes. Today, virtually everyone uses it in their daily cleansing routines. We use it in our ritual bathing and pour it over objects to purify or cleanse them. It is used in brew making, healing spells, or it can be drank in its pure state to help cleanse us within as well.

"Say these words: 'Messenger of Water, enter my blood and give the Water of Life to my body.' And you will feel, like the rushing current of the river, the power of the messenger of Water enter your blood and like the rivulets of a stream, send the power of the Earthly Mother through your blood to all the parts of your body."

Everyone agrees that drinking water gives your body energy for all its functions, including your thought and memory processes. Today we know that our bodies are made up of about 70% water. Some estimate the brain may be over 80% water and you need plenty of water to keep it working properly. When your brain is functioning on a full reserve of water, you'll be able to think faster, stay focused and experience a greater level of clarity and creativity. These are common, well known facts, with plenty of scientific evidence to back them up.

But there is also a spiritual aspect of water that few fully understand. In Wicca and many other nature-based beliefs, water represents emotions. It is considered a feminine energy and is thus associated with the Goddess. The element of water is believed to influence the conscious and the subconscious forces within us and is an important link in helping us connect with the Divine.

A few years ago I read an intriguing book called *The Hidden Messages in Water*. It explored a fascinating theory about water's deep connection to our individual and collective consciousness. In this book, Dr. Masaru Emoto describes how water can absorb, hold, and even retransmit human feelings and emotions!

He used high-speed photography to document changes in ice crystals when specific, concentrated thoughts were directed toward the water. Water exposed to loving words consistently showed brilliant, complex, and colorful snowflake patterns, just like the water from a clear spring, while water exposed to negative thoughts formed incomplete patterns with dull colors, similar to those formed by polluted water.

From these experiments he concluded that we may be able to heal our planet and ourselves by consciously expressing love and goodwill. This made a lot of sense to me. Over the centuries the Divine has been given credit for many miraculous healings that have no other explanation except that prayer or healing energies were sent to a person. Dr. Masaru Emoto's photography seemed to offer proof that thoughts or feelings could actually change water. If this is true, then a body that is 70% water is also likely to be transformed by the positive energies of thought and feeling.

To be clear, it is not a simple word or thought that transforms the water. Your words or thoughts must generate a deep feeling. It is your feelings that have the power to transform. When we feel deeply about something, that feeling can cause changes both within us and in the world around us.

We've all heard the phrase "sick with worry" and there is no question that being stressed or worried can have a negative effect on your health. Research has also documented that people who are happy and stress-free, tend to live longer healthier lives. Clearly our emotions do affect our health. So the idea that there is a connection between our thoughts and the effect they have on the water in our bodies seems quite logical.

It seems the Divine may have given all of us the ability to heal ourselves and others. When we are aware of how our thoughts and feelings affect the element of water, we are more likely to send forth energies that are loving, peaceful and full of gratitude. If we choose to feel hate, anger or even frustration, we must do so with the full knowledge that it is having a negative effect, not only on our own bodies, but on those around us as well.

The element of Water is a powerful emotional link to the Goddess. When you express deep feelings for something, she hears you loud and clear!

Water seems to be one of the most powerful elements when it comes to communicating with the Divine. The stronger our emotions are, the faster the response is. When you open this line up with love, gratitude and a peaceful heart, the Divine power of the Goddess flows easily into your life.

For further reading, I highly recommend *The Healing Power of Water* and *The Hidden Messages of Water*. Both books are by Masaru Emoto.

The Akashic Records and SPIRIT

"For the Son of Man is not all that he seems and only with the eyes of the spirit can we see those golden threads which link us with all life everywhere."

References to the Akashic records, also known as the Aether or the eternal Book of Life, date back to antiquity. They are sometimes described as a universal filing system that recorded every occurring thought, word, and action since the beginning of time. Today, scientists might think of this record as the DNA of the universe. It is a complete record of all that ever was.

"I tell you truly, the heavenly kingdoms are crossed and crossed again by streams of golden light, arching far beyond the dome of the sky and having no end."

In their writings, the Essenes described a Golden Web of Eternal Life. It was called eternal because the Golden threads of this web had no end. It encompassed not only everything on earth, but everything in the heavens as well. They knew only that it connected all things together and that by tapping into it, you could walk with the Angels or Messengers and learn the secrets of the Divine.

"And close your eyes, Sons of Light, and in sleep contemplate the oneness of all life everywhere. For I tell you truly, in the daylight hours are our feet on the ground and we have no wings with which to fly. But our spirits are not tied to the earth and with the coming of night we overcome our attachment to the earth and join with that which is eternal."

In these ancient texts, it was suggested that you could join with this eternal web as you slept. Many traditions teach that it is accessible by our subconscious mind, through a deep state of relaxation, meditation or dreams. It is something that you can connect with only when there is complete harmony between the body, mind and spirit. An uncluttered mind and a strong connection with one's Higher Self or Inner Spirit are needed.

Today, science is just starting to explore the idea that all things are connected by a field of energy. In the last couple of decades, a series of scientific experiments have actually revealed dramatic evidence of a web of energy. It suggests that all things may be connected through this energy field. Even when we are personally unaware of it, we are constantly interacting with the energy of everything around us and we are shaping our world with every thought and feeling, because our mind and body are not truly separate from the environment.

This new evidence supports the idea that each of us has the power to speak directly to the Divine force that connects all of creation.

Sadly, most people go about their day never realizing that everything they are thinking or feeling is being sent out through this web or energy field. They worry all day about their finances, job or relationships and then wonder why they are experiencing more money problems, stress on the job or problems at home. Their thoughts and feelings are simply attracting more of that same type of energy back into their lives.

If you are trying to communicate with the Goddess about what you want or need, go to her with a joyful spirit and express your gratitude for the gift she will be giving you. Allow your inner spirit or higher self to do the talking.

When you need to hear her voice and want to know what direction or steps to take next, a quiet mind is essential. Take a walk through the outdoors to clear your mind, practice a few minutes of meditation or listen to some relaxing music or nature sounds. You may want to keep a dream journal by your bed to record any unusual dreams or messages you receive in your sleep. Remember that you are linked with all living things and be alert to potential messages the Divine may send you through others.

Spirit is more than just the life-force within us. It is actually a network of energy and the sum total of every living thing that has ever existed!

If you would like to learn more about this amazing web of energy that links us all together, I recommend reading *The Divine Matrix* by Gregg Braden. He does a wonderful job of blending all the ancient teachings and traditions on this subject with the new scientific research that is being done today You may also enjoy *The*

Synchronicity Key: The Hidden Intelligence Guiding the Universe and You by David Wilcox or *The Field* by Lynne McTaggart

Being One With The Goddess

"With the eyes and ears of the spirit do you see and hear the sights and sounds of the kingdom of the Earthly Mother: the blue sky where dwells the messenger of Air, the foaming river where flows the messenger of Water, the golden light which streams from the messenger of Sun. And I tell you truly, all these are within you as well as without; for your breath, your blood, the fire of life within you, all are one with the Earthly Mother."

In these ancient manuscripts we are taught to use the eyes and ears of the spirit to hear the sights and sounds of the Earthly Mother or Goddess. For a long time I did not truly understand what this meant. Now I believe it is simply trying to tell us to look past the surface to see the Divine Spirit within all things and listen to our inner thoughts and feelings to hear the voice of the Divine. The Spirit is unseen, just as our thoughts and feelings are unseen. The Goddess sends her messages to our minds and our hearts. Watch for signs in nature and pay close attention to your thoughts and feelings in every situation. This is the Divine guiding your steps.

Spiritual leaders from many different traditions understand how to connect the Divine through nature. Interestingly enough, they are not the only ones with this knowledge. We are all born with a natural interest in the world around us. As children, we explore the magic of everything we see. We enjoy the fresh air and sunshine and love splashing in the water of a pool or playing in the sand and soil of Mother Earth. Perhaps if we did a little more this as adults that same magic would still be part of our lives.

The best book I ever read was written by a young girl named Opal Whiteley. When she was six and seven she kept a diary describing the world as she saw it, alive with creatures, fairies, talking trees, and singing creeks. Her writings were published in 1920 and are still being read today. I have selected a few quotes from her books to share with you. The wording can be a little odd at times, but this adds to the charm.

"When we were gone a little way on from the very tall trees, in the sky the light of day was going from blue to silver. And thoughts had coming down the road to meet us. They were thoughts from the mountains where are the mines. They were thoughts from the canyons that come down to meet the road by the river. I did feel their coming close about us. Very near they were and all about. We went on a little way only. We went very slow. We had listens to the thoughts. They were thoughts of blooming-time and coming-time. They were the soul thoughts of little things that soon will have their borning-time."

"The wind comes creeping in under the door. It calls, Come, come, petite Françoise , come. It calls to me to come go exploring. It sings of the things that are to be found under leaves. It whispers the dreams of the tall fir trees. It does pipe the gentle song the forest sings on gray days. I hear all the voices calling me. I listen "

"I went out the front door and a little way down the path. I made a stop to watch the clouds. They first did come over the hills in a slow way. Then they did sail on and on. They were like ships. I did have wonders what thoughts they were carrying from the hills to somewhere."

"Raindrops were beginning to come down from the sky. ...I watched the raindrops in the brook going on and on. When I grow up I am going to write a book about a raindrop's journey."

"As we did go along, we did have listens to the voices of the trees and grass. The girl that has no seeing is learning to have hearing of what the grasses say and of the waters of the brooks that tell the hill songs. Too, she is learning to see things. She shuts her eyes when I shut mine. We go on journeys together."

"And I do help her to get understandings of the thoughts growing with the flowers and the trees and the leaves. And I do tell her as how those are God's thoughts growing right up out of the earth."

When Opal said "we" she was often referring to one of her animal companions. However, in the last two quotes, Opal was trying to teach a blind girl to see and hear with the eyes and ears of the spirit. This is what we all need to learn!

The Goddess sends her messengers of Earth, Air, Fire and Water to whisper her secrets to you. These elements all work together to strengthen your spirit and draw you closer to the Divine.

Below is another excerpt from the Teachings of the Elect that tell us how Mother Earth's messengers work together to give life to small grains of wheat.

"And I did moisten a handful of wheat, that the messenger of Water entered into it. The messenger of Air did also embrace it, and the messenger of Sun, and the power of the three messengers awakened also the messenger of Life within the wheat, and sprout and root were born in each grain. Then I put the awakened wheat into the soil of the messenger of Earth, and the power of the Earthly Mother and all her messengers entered into the wheat, and when the sun had risen four times the grains had become grass. I tell you truly, there is no greater miracle than this."

In this beautiful story, the messengers of Earth, Air, Fire and Water bring the messenger of Life to the grains of wheat. Like the wheat, you can be awakened and the power of the Earthly Mother will enter you. when you commune with her messengers. They are all vital to the spirit. Try to spend some time with each on a daily basis if you want to strengthen your spirit and maximize your connection with the Goddess. The following excerpt from the Teachings of the Elect is very similar to the writings in the little girl's diary. It fascinates me that a child's words can reflect the same wise teachings as these spiritual leaders.

"It is the blood of our Earthly Mother which falls from the clouds and flows in the rivers; it is the breath of our

Earthly Mother which whispers in the leaves of the forest and blows with a mighty wind from the mountains; sweet and firm is the flesh of our Earthly Mother in the fruits of the trees; strong and unflinching are the bones of our Earthly Mother in the giant rocks and stones which stand as sentinels of the lost times; truly, we are one with our Earthly Mother, and he who clings to the laws of his Mother, to him shall his Mother cling also."

Secret Messages From Plants

"But of all these and more, that most precious gift of your Earthly Mother is the grass beneath your feet, even that grass which you tread upon without thought. Humble and meek is the messenger of Earth, for she has no wings to fly, nor golden rays of light to pierce the mist. But great is her strength and vast is her domain, for she covers the earth with her power, and without her the Sons of Men would be no more, for no man can live without the grass, the trees and the plants of the Earthly Mother. And these are the gifts of the messenger of Earth to the Sons of Men."

The spirits of trees, plants and grass call to each of us. Their energy resonates with us and through them, Mother Earth will happily share her secrets with us if we are willing to listen. Below are a few more quotes from Opal's diary about the messages the elements were sending her:

"I lay my ear close to the earth where the grasses grew close together. I did listen. The wind made ripples on the grass as it went over. There were voices from out the earth. And the things of their saying were the things of gladness of growing. And there was music. And in the music there was sky-twinkles and earth-tinkles . That was come of the joy of living. I have thinks all the grasses growing there did feel glad feels from the tips of their green arms to their toe roots in the ground."

"There by the dim trail grow the honeysuckles. I nod to them as I go that way. In the daytime I hear them talk with sunbeams and the wind. They talk in shadows with the little people of the sun. And this I have learned -- grown-ups do not know the language of shadows."

"I went goes on, to pull weeds by the bean-folks . I went back some steps to look looks at them. Those bean-folks in the garden are such climbers. Their thoughts reach up toward the sky. And they climb up on the poles we put in the garden there."

"The sun was up and the birds were singing. I went my way. As I did go, I did have hearing of many voices. They were the voices of earth glad for the spring. They did say what they had to say in the growing grass and in the leaves growing out from tips of branches. The birds did

have knowing and sang what the grasses and leaves did say of the gladness of living. I too, did feel glad feels from my toes to my curls."

It may be those "glad feels" that we miss the most as adults. In our busy, hectic life we forget to pause and listen to the voices of our Mother Earth. The Goddess is constantly whispering her secrets to us, but we cannot hear when our thoughts are on our finances, jobs and daily challenges. Go sit outside in the grass, feel the wind on your face and the sun on your shoulders. The goddess's voice is much easier to hear when you are surrounded by nature.

"Here is the secret, Sons of Light; here in the humble grass. Here is the meeting place of the Earthly Mother and the Heavenly Father; here is the Stream of Life which gave birth to all creation; I tell you truly, only to the Son of Man is it given to see and hear and touch the Stream of Life which flows between the Earthly and Heavenly Kingdoms. Place your hands around the tender grass of the messenger of Earth, and you will see and hear and touch the power of all the messengers."

The Stream of Life is mentioned numerous times in these ancient manuscripts. It refers to the Divine power or energy that flows through all living things. It is the eternal web of life, the golden threads that link all things in this world and beyond. It's important to realize that we are all part of this Stream of Life. All of our thoughts, feelings and actions send ripples through this stream and whatever type of energy we send out will be multiplied and drawn back into our lives.

Messages From Animals

The Goddess speaks to us through the natural world. Sometimes it is through the elements and other times it is through the plants and animals around us. We are all part of the this world and the more we understand it, the more we understand ourselves.

To understand the messages that animals can bring us, it helps to know a little about each one. If you were planning to vacation in another country, you would probably try to learn a little of the native language. The more familiar you become with the language, the easier it will be for you find your way around and the trip becomes much more enjoyable. The more you know about the animals around you, the easier it will be to pick up on the messages they bring you.

Animals have a great deal to teach us. Some are great parents and protectors, others are experts at survival and then there are those who will simply teach us how to be playful or more loving. Our ancestors had a close connection to the wildlife in nature. They would learn the "language" of an animal and thus knew what message the Divine was sending them when the animal appeared.

Sometimes an animal can warn us that a harsh winter is approaching. Other times it may bring a message that Spring is near. Some say that birds have led him lead them to food and water or helped them find their way when they became lost. Certain animals bring a message of strength or courage, while others tell us to relax and enjoy life. Again, the more we learn about our animal friends, the easier it will be for them to communicate with us.

In the best-selling book Animal Speak, Ted Andrews tells us:

"When we learn to speak with the animals, to listen with animal ears and to see through animal eyes, we experience the phenomena, the power and the potential of the human essence, and it is then that the animals are no longer our subordinates. They become our teachers, our friends, and our companions. They show us the true majesty of life itself. They restore our forgotten childlike wonder at the world and the reawaken our lost lead in magic, dreams and possibilities."

Every living creature contains an aspect of the Divine power within it. Wiccans, Shamans and followers of nature-based traditions are well aware of this connection. They know the threads in the web of life link the invisible and visible worlds and they understand that animals and all living things speak to those who listen. Ultimately, every species and every aspect of its environment reminds us of what we can manifest in our own lives.

Sometimes we will have personal contact with a special animal, but other times it comes to us in our dreams, or we see images of it everywhere. When an animal draws our attention, we need to ask ourselves what qualities that animal is bringing to us. An animal can be a symbol of a specific power or energy manifesting In your life.

Remember the old sayings: clever as a fox, wise as an owl or strong as an ox? These are traditional animal symbols. What that animal symbolizes to YOU is what matters most. Sit down and meditate about the animal. Think about why it is appearing in your life. Learn more about it from books, online or visit it in its own environment when possible.

Here is a short list of a few common animals and what they traditionally symbolize:

Butterflies symbolize joy, freedom, living in the moment, transformation

Cats can symbolize cunning, agility, aloofness, independence and seeing spirits.

Dogs are service-oriented protectors. For many, they symbolize loyalty, friendship and unconditional love.

Deer can symbolize gentleness, grace, swiftness, abundance, intuition and alternative paths to a goal.

Hawks are observant and perceptive messengers from the spirit world. They can symbolize the ability to see the big picture and teach you to use your personal talents.

Hummingbirds symbolize freedom of movement, energy, tireless joy and living from life's nectar.

Owls symbolize wisdom and the ability to see things that are hidden.

Raccoons can symbolize ingenuity, generosity, caring for others and the ability to adapt.

Ravens are a symbol of magic, the spirit world and changes in consciousness

Wolves symbolize family, teaching, co-operation, insight, strength, leadership, loyalty, freedom and psychic energy connected to the moon.

If you would like to read a little more about animals and what messages they may be bringing you, visit the Animal Symbology pages on our website. http://wicca.com/celtic/wyldkat/wklist.html

you may also enjoy reading *Animal Speak* by Ted Andrews. If you are interested in learning more about the messages animals bring you, that's a great place to start.

The Power Of Intuition

Intuition is your line of communication to the Divine. It's the ability of the mind to know or sense without the use of rational processes. This ability has also been referred to as a gut-feeling, your inner-voice, your higher-self, or even your guardian angel. The name you give this quiet voice within really doesn't matter, as long as you understand that this is how the Goddess often communicates with you. Learning to listen to and follow your intuition can provide you with Divine wisdom and guidance as you face the challenges of everyday life.

In the military, a line of communication is used to connect a unit with its supply base. This open line of communication is vital for military units to operate effectively. We may not be in the military, but we can't avoid the mundane battles of daily life, and having an open line of communication to the Divine can be very helpful when it comes to getting supplies and reinforcements!

There is no doubt that developing your intuition can increase your success in life. The Goddess provides plenty of signs along the way to guide you. You must learn to watch for these signs and let your intuition or inner-voice interpret them for you. A number of unfortunate events might indicate you are headed in the wrong direction, while a fortunate coincidence can indicate you are on the right path. Always trust what your intuition tells you.

Divine intuition is usually easy to identify. First, when something is right for you, you'll feel good about the thoughts you are having and the idea will seem right and/or make you happy inside. Second, if for any reason you are uncertain about a course you are meant to take, you can count on the Divine to send you multiple signs. The Goddess will encourage you with various reminders to gently turn you in the right direction. Multiple signs, along with positive thoughts and/or feelings about something, should leave little room for doubt that you're on the right path.

Developing Your Abilities

When you learn to follow your intuition, you can create a life with less stress and more good fortune. It's a simple matter of watching for the signs and trusting your intuition to guide you. As you learn to do this, you'll start finding yourself in the right place at the right time, and connecting with people who can help you. You'll stop HOPING for the things you need ... and start EXPECTING to find them, because you know that the Goddess is at work in your life!

Don't be shy about asking for signs if you need them. The Goddess will always be happy to give them to you. When I began to study this path, all the signs pointed me in the same direction. However, I continued to ask for more guidance, because I was heading down a new path and I wanted to be SURE it was right for me. I asked for so many signs that I was afraid the Divine would consider me a lost cause and give up trying to guide me.

Luckily, it doesn't work that way. The Goddess is very patient. She will send you as many signs as you need, until you feel totally comfortable with the direction you are going. Just let your intuition help you read the signs. Consider how you FEEL about the direction the signs are pointing to. With practice you'll learn to recognize signs and be more confident in your response.

I can't tell you what signs to watch for, because your path is different from mine. The roads you travel on your journey will depend on where you are now and what your interests and abilities are. Your intuition works a lot like a GPS (Global Positioning System) to help you navigate. It will faithfully suggest the best route to get you to your destination. The signs you see along the way will either confirm that you are going in the right direction, or they will let you know that you took a wrong turn. You are always free to choose another road, but learning to follow the guidance of your intuition can make your journey through life easier and much more enjoyable!

Below are two important "navigation tips" that will ensure you have a wonderful journey:

First, take your focus off of your personal wants or needs. This can be hard to do, but if your thoughts and actions reflect this type of energy, you are likely to draw more want and need into your life. Instead, make your journey about finding ways to help others. In return, the Goddess will make sure you have all the help YOU need.

Share any gifts you have already been given, and you will be given more. You simply can't out-give the Divine Power of the Universe. Your life will always be blessed as the joy, peace and love you give away is multiplied and returned to you. But to receive, you must first be willing to give. This is also known as the Universal Law of Attraction, the Law of Three or the Law of Return.

Second, express gratitude for everything. Be thankful for what you currently have, what you can do now, and who you are today. It's easy to take little things for granted, but an ungrateful heart tends to block the flow of Divine energy. If you don't show appreciation for the blessings you are given, you risk losing them.

Think about the areas of your life that are currently fruitful. You have most likely expressed your gratitude for these things. This is easy to do. However, areas of your life that seem to be lacking or unfruitful are harder to give thanks for. If your roof is leaking, be thankful that you still have shelter. If your car has seen better days, give thanks that at least you don't have to walk miles to get to work ... or if you DO have to walk, be grateful that you have the ability to walk and/or a job to walk to. Have you been sick? Give thanks that you are alive to experience the beauty of the world around you. Don't reserve gratitude just for the big things. Keep the Divine energy flowing through your life by also giving thanks for any areas of your life that seem to be lacking ... then relax, and watch these areas become fruitful again. Expressing sincere gratitude for everything allows Divine energy to flow freely through all aspects of your life, and the Universal Three-fold Law will start working to provide you with a never-ending supply of things to be thankful for!

Communicating With Divination Tools

Divination usually involves the use of an object or objects to gain answers to questions, or to see events, that are not perceptible to the average person. The use of interpretive tools can help the Divine relay guidance through your inner spirit or higher-self. This is a common practice among Wiccans, Witches, and other Pagans. Divination takes many forms, and while some of the Craft will use several different techniques, most everyone has their own favorite method for seeking answers from the Divine.

Some of the favorite divination methods include the use of tarot cards, pendulums or runes. Crystal and/or crystal ball gazing, reading tea leaves, gazing into a pool or bowl of water or candle gazing are also popular. The list goes on and on.

Any of these items can help you strengthen your intuition. Simply choose the one you are most comfortable using and practice,

practice, practice. It may seem hard in the beginning, but don't give up. The more you use these tools, the easier it gets.

Think of your divination tools as exercise equipment for your intuition. If you want to strengthen your body, you might choose a treadmill, bicycle or weights to help you achieve your goal. Some of this equipment can prove challenging when you first start to work with it, but the more you use it, the stronger your body will become. If you want to develop your intuition or spiritual self, divination tools can be a tremendous help.

Almost anything can be used as a divination tool, and over the centuries just about everything has been. You are simply using these items to strengthen your spirit or intuition. Don't overwhelm yourself. Start with tools you are comfortable with and try more complicated methods as you develop your abilities.

Sometimes divination is described as fortune-telling. If you think it is simply an attempt to find out about future events before they happen, think again! Its real value is that it can help you plan for, and prevent outcomes. If you like the answers you receive, you can continue on your current path. If it warns you of trouble ahead, you can adjust your course of action, and thus change the outcome. In this way, divination can provide you with Divine guidance that allows you to make better choices and have a higher level of control over your future.

Divination is about communicating WITH the Divine and seeking Divine wisdom. It is like connecting with a wise old friend who can offer you Divine guidance on anything and everything you want to talk about. Your intuition or higher-self will always guide you to options that are best for you.

If your intuition detects a negative sign, it doesn't mean something bad is destined to happen. Most often, this is a clue to a thought or action that is causing a roadblock on your path, or an issue that you need to deal with. Pay attention to what your intuition is telling you, and use the information to make better choices in your life. Use your Divine intuition freely. This amazing blessing is available to all of us and it's intended for daily use!

To get you started, here is a reprint of an article on Crystal Ball Gazing, courtesy of The Celtic Connection

Crystal Ball Gazing

http://wicca.com

This technique is best if done with a Crystal Ball 2-5 inches in diameter and works best on nights of the full moon. If the purchase of a Crystal Ball is not within your budget, a bowl of water with a Quartz Crystal Cluster at the bottom will suffice. True Quartz Crystal Balls can be quite expensive. Also, never substitute a resin or glass ball since they are ineffective for anything other than children's games.

Light one or two candles in a darkened, quiet room. You can hold the crystal or place it on a stand, but it should have a blue or black velvet cloth underneath it. Make sure that there are no reflections from anything showing in the ball. You can also burn incense if you wish. Patchouli works great for me.

Before beginning, center yourself. Gaze into the ball, but do not stare. Try not to blink that much. While you are gazing, breathe in and out slowly and deeply. Just relax and gaze. You will feel a sense of limitless time. Enjoy the peacefulness and simply gaze. Do this for at least 15 minutes, and increase your time by 5 minutes with each succeeding session.

Usually around the second or third session, you will notice a small cloudy glow in the center of the crystal. This is your focusing area where your visions will appear. You may get a vision on your first try, while others have to attempt it several times before seeing something. Go at your own pace.

It is best to just gaze and receive whatever comes to you. There are different forms that visions come in. You may get actual visions of places and people, or you may get symbolic pictures.

One form that visions come in are colored clouds. Although no one has been successful in identifying what each color cloud means, the following has been pretty accurate for a lot of seers.

Blue clouds symbolize success of career or business

Gold clouds symbolize prosperity, steady cash flow, and renewed romance to come

Gray/Dark gray symbolize ill fortune

Black clouds symbolize some seriously bad stuff coming one's way

Green clouds symbolize health, happiness of the heart

Orange clouds symbolize hidden aggression and anger, troubled emotions

Red clouds symbolize danger to come. This person must watch themselves

Silver clouds symbolize troublesome times ahead followed by goodness

White clouds symbolize very good fortune to come

Yellow clouds symbolize upcoming obstacles

As with most other topics, it is impossible to cover all the forms of divination in one chapter. Entire books have been written on each method. For further reading you can try **Divination for Beginners by Scott Cunningham or Tarot for Beginners by Lisa Chamberlain**. Both are clearly written and easy to understand divination guides.

Enjoy!

Meditation

"Do not think because it cannot be seen, that thought has no power. I tell you truly, the lightning that cleaves the mighty oak, or the quaking that opens up cracks in the earth, these are as the play of children compared with the power of thought."

This topic was saved for last because as you begin to explore the path on your own, you'll find this can be an excellent first step. Meditation has been an important part of religious traditions and beliefs since ancient times. It teaches us how to control our thoughts, and this is critical if you hope to live a magical life.

You know that the thoughts you send forth will determine how the Universe responds to you. You also know that positive thoughts and energy sent forth tend to draw positive energy back into your life three-fold. If you allow the thoughts you send out to uplift others, the Divine will uplift and refresh your energy as well. Do your best to avoid all negative thoughts.

"Truly each thought of darkness, whether of malice or anger or vengeance, these wreak destruction like that of fire sweeping through dry kindling under a windless sky."

We do not always see the full harm caused by our negative thoughts and energy. Many think that negative thoughts are not really harmful as long as they are not spoken or acted upon. Unfortunately, they can still have a very destructive influence, and because of this, every effort should be made to keep the mind positive.

Learning to control our thoughts offers many benefits, not only for the mind, but for the body and spirit as well. In over 1,000 published research studies, meditation has been linked to changes in brain activity, blood pressure, metabolism, and other processes of the body. It has been used in clinical settings as a method of stress and pain reduction. The mind is clearly one of our most powerful assets.

Practitioners of Wicca and Witchcraft will tell you that magic is the art and science of changing states of mind at will. Meditation can help you train your mind and transform it from negative to positive, from stressed to peaceful, or from unhappy to happy. Your goal should be to overcome negative thinking and cultivate constructive thoughts before proceeding with any magical or spellwork.

By training in meditation, you can create an inner peace and clarity that enables you to control your mind regardless of the external circumstances.

You'll find several breathing and meditation techniques below to help you get started. There are numerous forms of meditation. You'll need to research and study the various methods combining this with experimentation to discover which will ultimately work best for you.

The Quiet Mind

The main purpose of this meditation is to stop distractions and make your mind clearer and more lucid. Choose a quiet place to meditate and sit in a comfortable position on the floor or in a chair. Your back should be as straight as possible, as this helps keep your mind alert. Begin to focus on your breathing. Your thoughts should be on the sensation of the breath as it enters and leaves your nostrils. Just breathe naturally and try to concentrate on your breathing to the exclusion of everything else.

At first, your mind may be very busy. You may be tempted to follow the different thoughts as they arise, but resist this and remain focused on the sensation of your breath. If you discover your mind has wandered and is following your thoughts, simply return it to the breath. Repeat this as many times as necessary until your mind settles on your breathing. Even ten or fifteen minutes of this simple meditation can be helpful in quieting the mind and relieving stress from your day. It's a great place to start. It will get easier with practice, and you can then move on to other methods of meditation if you like.

A Centering Meditation

Sit any way that you feel comfy, so long as your spine is straight.

Close your eyes and focus on your breathing. Take very long and very deep breaths through your nose.

Each time you breathe in, hold it for 2 or 3 seconds and then slowly exhale. Continue this breathing until you feel very calm and peaceful. This usually takes 3-5 minutes, but take as long as you need. It is different for everyone. Just go at your own pace.

You can also use sound to center yourself. Just sit quietly and ring a small bell or chimes. Focus on the soft sound and breathe deeply. Keep making the noise until you feel centered.

A Grounding Technique

This works great for those times in school or at work when you just can't seem to keep your feet still or relax.

Place your feet flat on the floor and breathe in deeply. On the exhale, picture the excess energy flowing out of your feet and into the Earth.

Keep doing this until you feel calm. Usually my feet feel very heavy after doing this. My friends have gotten the same feeling too, so I guess it is just a normal sensation.

How To Find A Mantra That Fits You

A mantra is a word or sound repeated to aid concentration in meditation.

To find your personal mantra, sit in a comfy position. Picture yourself leaving your body and travel up to the cosmos.

See yourself sitting calmly in the center of the Universe. Concentrate on the stars, then after a few minutes of gazing at them, a few of the stars will glow a bright baby blue.

Concentrate on one bright blue star at a time. As you gaze at that particular star, you may hear a phrase or word whispered in your head. Repeat what you hear and focus inward. If the mantra is right for you, you will know it within. If it is not right for you, simply gaze at another blue star and repeat this until you find a mantra that fits you.

After you find a mantra, thank the Universe and feel yourself slowly descending from the sky, back into your body.

When you open your eyes, you might feel a little tired or drained. I find that drinking a nice cold cup of juice re-energizes my body. You might also wish to have a small snack. Milk and juice are ideal for recharging yourself.

Pranayama

Pranayama is the formal practice of controlling the breath. It brings more oxygen to the blood and brain and helps control Prana, our vital life energy. The word is composed of two Sanskrit words: prana, which means life force, or vital energy, (also known as the breath), and *ayāma*, which means to extend or draw out. The main purpose of pranayama is to relax the body and mind.

There are many kinds of pranayama and the more advanced techniques should only be done under the supervision of an expert, since working with breath can unleash powerful forces or energies in the body and mind.

However, there is a popular technique called the Four Fold Breath that can calm and "ground" a practitioner, helping them prepare for meditation and rituals. This is the simplest rhythm for the beginner.

The focus is on regular breathing. Simply inhale to a count of four, hold for a count of four, exhale for a count of four, and hold with empty lungs for a count of four. Repeat the entire process. How fast or slow you count is not important. Find a rhythm that works for you and allows you to feel comfortable and relaxed. Once you have attained this, continue for a minute or two, or until you are completely quieted and relaxed. You may then proceed with your meditation or ritual work.

There should be no strain of any kind during your pranayama. Begin with a minute or two a day for the first week and gradually increase up to five minutes a day.

If you do this simple pranayama technique before your magical activity, it will help you to get 'into the mood'. It is also an excellent aid to relaxation, tension release and centering yourself.

"He who hath found peace with the mind, hath learned to soar beyond the realm of the Angels. Know this peace with thy mind, desire this peace with thy heart, fulfill this peace with thy body." The Sevenfold Peace

For further reading on the topics of meditation I recommend Meditation for Beginners - How to Relieve Stress, Anxiety and Depression and Return to a State of Inner Peace and Happiness by Yesenia Chavan

If you would like to give yoga a try, a great place to start is with The Heart of Yoga: Developing a Personal Practice by T. K. V. Desikachar

Walking With The Goddess

Will you live your life differently knowing the Goddess is responding to ALL your thoughts and feelings? As you talk with her daily, you'll soon discover that you have the power within you to create joy, heal suffering and bring peace to the world around you.

Wicca and other nature-based paths are dynamic and intuitive. It is simply something you must experience to truly understand.

Reading lots of books is a great way to get started, but trying to learn about Wicca and the old ways from books, is like trying to taste your food by looking at a pictures of it. It will never be truly satisfying.

You are communing with the natural forces of this Universe, and learning how to do this takes time. It is not something that can be mastered in a few short weeks, or even a few short years. It is a path that offers an ongoing, never-ending learning experience to those who follow it.

As I began to write this chapter, I received an email from a young reader who felt "stuck" on her journey. This person had read a number of books and felt she was no longer picking up any new information. If you choose to continue on this path, and you find yourself stuck or not moving forward, it may be that you are too focused on the religion itself.

Don't limit your journey to simply learning the traditions and practices of your path. Wicca is so much more! It's about connecting with the Earth and everything around you. Don't be afraid to venture out and explore the areas that draw your interest. Your Mother Earth offers more secrets and mysteries than you can absorb in a lifetime, and she is happy to share them with those who seek her wisdom.

As you continue your journey, there will be times when your work or family activities will demand extra attention. These events may tempt you to put your spiritual needs on hold, but there are many ways to stay connected that take very little effort.

If you can't find time for formal rituals and celebrations, stay connected in small ways. Turn to your Mother Earth and allow her to lift your spirit by walking barefoot in the cool grass, or relaxing for a few minutes as you sit in the shade of a giant tree.

If you can't get outdoors, bring a living plant inside to remind you of the gifts the Earth provides you. A small tabletop fountain can bring the element of water indoors. Anything that reminds you of nature will help you stay connected to your Mother Earth, even when life is extra chaotic. It is during these times that you need the most help. Stay connected!

While there are no magic words to protect you from all the negative energy in this world, in Wicca, the Divine will use your connection to Mother Earth to give you all the strength you need to deal with what comes your way.

And while there is no spell that can make money magically appear before you, the Universal Law of Return can be used to enrich your life in many wonderful ways. It is limited only by your own thoughts and actions.

Keep in mind that you must first give if you hope to receive. If you want more love in your life, start sending more love out to those around you. Love is bound to return to you three-fold.

Do your best to follow the Harm None Rule of the Wiccan Rede. These Universal Laws are the foundation Wicca is built on. They can be applied to most any path you choose to walk and should be followed to the best of your ability.

Finally, some practitioners tend to focus on working with a specific element. Most of us have a predominate element that we feel drawn to and there is nothing wrong with that. However, it's always good to learn to work in harmony with each of the elements. The more elements you commune with, the stronger your connection with the Goddess will be.

Communing daily with the elements of Earth, Air, Fire and Water will strengthen your body, mind and spirit. Good health, a sharper mind and a joyful heart are just a few of the blessings you can experience on this path. With a strong connection to the Goddess and everything around you, your life will feel more magical than ever. Enjoy the journey!

Increasing Your Magical Energy

No matter what path we choose to walk, Mother Earth has an effect on our lives. We have all been refreshed by the feel of soft grass beneath our feet, the fresh outdoor air and the warmth of the sun on our face or the cool waters of a lake or stream.

"Always have the Brothers of Light lived where rejoice the angels of the Earthly Mother: near rivers, near trees, near flowers, near the music of birds; where sun and rain may embrace the body, which is the temple of the spirit." The Teachings of the Elect

Most are satisfied with this natural exchange of energy, and they will go outdoors to recharge whenever they find time to. But in Wicca, you can learn methods to draw on and amplify this Divine energy whenever you need it.

As you learn how to work with this energy, always be respectful of the powers and spirits of our Mother Earth. You are not trying to control the forces of nature and bend them to your will. You are simply working WITH them to influence the direction they flow through your life.

If you are raising energy for spellwork or magical purposes, you know how important it is to follow the Harm None rule and remember the Three-fold Law. To consistently ensure the best results, you may also want to focus your work on what you can GIVE to the Earth and those around you.

As the three-fold law teaches, the more positive energy you send out, the more you get back. You simply can't out-give the Universe. Thoughts and energy sent forth from a giving or loving heart will always multiply and return to you in kind.

On the other hand, if you allow your mind to simply focus on what you need or want, you may end up multiplying your needs and wants. This is why many get discouraged with spellwork and magic. They send forth the wrong type of thoughts and energy and then wonder why the results were not what they expected. *Keep in mind that anytime you worry about negative or harmful energies, you give them added power.* If you worry too much, you can actually draw more negative energy into your life.

So, as you begin any energy work, if you want positive results, always make sure you are sending forth positive thoughts AND feelings. Fill your mind with peaceful and relaxing images. Imagine what it feels like to already have the results you desire. Without clear, positive thoughts that generate positive feelings, negative energies can easily slip in and affect your results.

Finally, don't expect magical results to happen overnight. With a strong will and solid visualization skills, you can achieve what others believe is impossible. But, as with the muscles in your physical body, the strength of your thoughts or mind must be developed over time.

It will take practice. The more you exercise your visualization skills, the stronger your mind becomes. The stronger your mind or intent is, the more effective your magic will be. Some will find it easier than others, but ALL are capable of developing these skills!

Thank You!

If you found this book helpful, please help me share this information with others by posting a short review on Amazon. Your review really does make a difference! Reader feedback has always been my greatest source of inspiration and motivation to keep writing. I read all the reviews personally and use your comments to give you more of what you want.

Peace and health be with you,

Kardia

Additional Resources

To receive a FREE subscription to the Inner Circle Newsletter visit: http://wicca.com/publications/free.html This complimentary publication explores the ancient spiritual wisdom of Wicca, Witchcraft and Pagan traditions and it keeps you updated on any helpful new articles or books we publish about the Old Ways. **Welcome to the Inner Circle!**

The Celtic Connection offers a magical home to all who are seeking a spiritual connection with Nature and our Mother Earth. You can explore links to several hundred pages about Wicca and Witchcraft traditions, Paganism, Shamanism and the Old Ways. You'll also find information on Pagan holidays, moon phases, candle magic, healing herbs, animal guides, meditation and more. Then get the Pagan books, Wiccan jewelry, gifts and magical supplies you need in our Wicca stores. Please explore freely. Thank you for your interest in Wicca and the Old Ways.

http://wicca.com

If you're on Facebook, visit our Living Wicca Today page at: https://facebook.com/living.wicca.today This is a great place to connect with others who practice the Old Ways!

Books By Kardia Zoe

Book #1 Living Wicca Today: Wiccan & Pagan Holidays

Book # 2 Wicca: A Beginner's Guide to Earth Magic

Book #3 Wicca: A Beginner's Guide to Casting Spells

Book #4 Talking to the Goddess: Improving Your Connection With the Divine

Book Set - Volume 1: Pagan Holidays and Earth Magic Paperback Edition

Book Set – Volume 2: Casting Spells and Talking to the Goddess Paperback Edition

About The Author

Kardia Zoe is a native Oregonian and co-founder of one of the oldest and largest information sites for Wicca and Witchcraft on the Internet. The website averages over 2,000 unique visitors per day and she has been providing these guests with guidance since 1997. You can visit her site at http://wicca.com

Now, in her Living Wicca Today series, Kardia is sharing her years of insight into this beautiful Earth religion, as she addresses the most frequently asked questions about Wicca and gives you a clear, accurate understanding of the traditional beliefs and practices. Her books dispel the lingering myths and misconceptions that surround this religion, so you can move forward with confidence on an amazing journey into the enchanted world of Wicca.

11361829R00064

Printed in Great Britain
by Amazon